# NEW-SCHOOL

# LEADERSHIP

*Making a Difference in the*

*21st Century*

# D.A. ABRAMS

**D.A. Abrams**

# PRAISE FOR *NEW-SCHOOL LEADERSHIP*

"*New-School Leadership* provides a road map toward the transformational leadership I have watched D.A. Abrams manifest in responding to numerous challenges in business and in life, over the many years I have called him friend and colleague. This book is his gift to all of our toolsheds so that we may internalize and master the skills for ourselves."

—Honorable David N. Dinkins
106ᵗʰ Mayor of the City of New York

◆◆◆

"I have known D.A. for many years through his work at USTA, and in this book he draws upon decades of business experience to state explicit directions that will improve an individual's leadership skills. With the ever-changing nature of contemporary industry—whether for-profit, government or non-profit—his words serve as a lodestone to take your leadership to the next level, to make you a 'leader, version 2.0.'"

—Jeanne Moutoussamy-Ashe, Photographer
Founder & Chairman, Arthur Ashe Learning Center

◆ ◆ ◆

"Over the past decade, I have had the pleasure of interacting with D.A. and several of the teams he has led. He truly exemplifies the principles and attributes described in "The New School Leadership." He personally embraces continuous learning and growth, encourages innovation and has the insight and know-how to set clear expectations and make success a team sport. This book will provide you with the tools and confidence to excel as a leader."

—Rona D. Weinstein, Founding Principal
Prism Consulting Group LLC
Consultant, Executive Coach and Author
*De-Stress Yourself! Survive & Thrive in the Fast Lane*

♦ ♦ ♦

"I have added this to my collection of 'go to' books for leadership principles and ideas. D.A. has done a great job of marrying tried and true leadership practices with personal experiences. The notion that leadership success is a team sport is spot-on because individuals, not groups, are publicly lauded for their leadership skills, abilities and results. Harnessing the power of the group is an important lesson that D.A. has challenged anyone interested in becoming a successful leader to think about."

—Carlton Yearwood, Principle, True Blue Inclusion

♦ ♦ ♦

"As an Inclusion Director, I ascribe to a philosophy that leaders are MADE not born, and D.A. Abrams' book on New-School Leadership provides those individuals seeking to become leaders with clear, practical strategies and examples on how to be the very best. The author delivers a strategic framework that takes from the past, while infusing a 'new-school' model with 'must haves' on leadership."

—Kimberly Ford, Director of Inclusion, National Collegiate Athletic Association

♦♦♦

"An informative and intriguing read, *New-School Leadership* captures the essentials for contemporary leadership, inviting new leaders for business, associations, chambers and teams."

—Bob Harris, Chair, Harris Mgmt. Group; NonprofitCenter.com

♦♦♦

"D.A. Abrams defines and demonstrates 'New-School Leadership' with a substance of inspiring and progressive flair. The reader feels involved and empowered by this magnetic page-turner. I knew what was missing in today's various leadership models, and hoped Mr. Abrams' book would have the solutions. He delivered."

—Sonia E. Wilson, Fundraising & Publicity
Consultant, Development Specialist
Medgar Evers College (CUNY)

◆ ◆ ◆

"D.A. Abrams has written another book that is an inspiration to continue to become a better leader in the many facets that one travels along the road of life. His book qualifies and quantifies the 'new-school leadership model.' Well done!"

—Ann Koger, Haverford College Head Coach of
Women's Tennis and Associate Director of Athletics

◆ ◆ ◆

"I've known D.A. for decades, from before he took over the reins of the Eastern Tennis Association and now, as Chief Diversity and Inclusion Officer for the entire United States Tennis Association. His levelheaded, balanced approach to leadership was honed under the tutelage of our mutual friend, Henry Talbert. D.A. has developed into an innovative leader and his new book, *New-School Leadership*, is literally a manual on the effective management of people, maybe the most difficult job in the world."

—Bob Davis, CEO, The Panda Foundation, Inc.

◆ ◆ ◆

"You read books like this all the time and take away bits and pieces, but are always left wondering, does this person really practice what they are preaching? D.A. Abrams and his success are the living proof of all of his lessons on leadership in this book. These tried-and-true methods and philosophy have proven themselves. This is a must-read for everyone in business no matter what level you are at now. This book will help get you to the next! Thank you for writing a smart, contemporary book on leadership!"

—Michelle Wilson, Managing Partner, the b'elle group

◆ ◆ ◆

"I have known D.A. Abrams over thirty years. D.A. brings credibility to this very timely examination of leadership based on his experience, longevity, ability to overcome adversity, personal and professional success. D.A.'s comprehensive approach will lead to solutions that are more current and relevant to today's issues. The concepts in this book will help anyone who aspires to be an effective community and business leader in today's culture!"

—Derrick L. Alford, CEO, Registered Financial Consultant, FISCAL FITNESS TAX & FINANCIAL SERVICES, INC.

D.A. Abrams

◆◆◆◆◆◆

# TABLE OF CONTENTS

# FOREWORD

Millions of people around the world on any given day are engaged in the study of leadership. There is probably no subject more widely considered, analyzed and studied in the halls of academia, business, and government. We are all fascinated by the idea of leadership. That's because we know an effective leader fully engaged in their chosen cause will bring clarity of purpose, and meaningful change through their commitment to getting results. Dynamic leaders have made the difference throughout history, whether it's the leadership of Abraham Lincoln, Gandhi, Winston Churchill or Dr. Martin Luther King.

While there are many rich examples of extraordinary leadership, there has always been a divide between what we see exhibited by larger-than-life figures and our own efforts to find the path to nuts and bolts leadership required day-to-day in business, organizations, and communities. Great leaders are inspiring—but what happens behind the scenes? Often the task of practical leadership, that is, not just inspiring others, but getting things done, can seem beyond the scope of our capacity.

Despite volumes written about leadership and our preoccupation with the subject, we continue to struggle with the notion of becoming better leaders ourselves. We wonder what practical steps we must take and what personal habits must be developed. In the abstract it's easy to understand the personality characteristics, decisions, and attributes that have made historic leaders so revered. They've been well analyzed for decades, for us all to absorb. In reality, becoming an authentic leader in our own lives, careers, and businesses, requires more than an attempt to duplicate the celebrated approach of the masters.

There's another challenge. Leadership can take many forms. It can mean speaking out on a subject, and making a persuasive case. Or, it can also mean illustrating by example. It can mean being hands-on and mobilizing groups of people. Or, it can mean being silent when everyone else is loud and agitated. Leaders can be charismatic, or they can merely speak through their writing and actions. In other words, leadership can take on multiple forms, which is why the subject can be so intimidating and misunderstood.

I have often wondered how many individuals striving to become better leaders realize the complexities of leadership and how modern shifts in our thinking, work, and tools have drastically changed the practice of leadership from the times those legendary leaders we all admire were prominent.

At its core, the idea of leadership has not changed, but the way a leader emerges and the tactics used by leaders have morphed steadily since technologies like television became mainstream in the 1950s.

You have to wonder: would the Civil Rights movement (and thus the leadership of Dr. Martin Luther King and President Lyndon Johnson) have been as effective had there not been images of injustice seared into our consciousness by television?

Would the Soviet Union have toppled had the words "Evil Empire" voiced by President Ronald Reagan not been carried worldwide by radio and television broadcasts, and had there not been the threat of the theoretical new technology of the Strategic Defense Initiative?

Would the revolutionary wave of demonstrations and protests known as the Arab Spring have occurred had civil resistance not been aided by a network of mobile phones, digital cameras, and social media websites?

Would Barack Obama have been elected the first African-American president of the United States had we not been able to observe and understand him in more intimate terms, aided by the wide spread broadcast of his speeches, and the reflection and commentary of millions on social media?

The fact is, today, new leadership models have taken shape which have been advanced by the ongoing emergence of new technologies and our willingness to adopt them.

It isn't just technology that has made the difference. Just look, for example, at the leadership of women in business today. We've got a long way to go, but powerful leaders like Mary Barra at General Motors, Gina Rometty at IBM, Sheryl Sandberg at Facebook, Marissa Mayer at Yahoo, and Ursula Burns at Xerox are reshaping our view of what and how women can lead.

There is also the role of global competition. What is an American automobile today? What is an American garment today? These are products sold in the United States that may not be designed, nor fully made in the U.S. and not necessarily by Americans. Industry collaboration, immigration, and the practicalities of business demand that we redefine what it means to lead even when it comes to industries where U.S. manufacturing leadership was once unquestionable. In this case understanding the intangibles of leadership is key.

In this powerful book, *New-School Leadership*, my good friend D.A. Abrams examines new paradigms in leadership, and distills the ingredients of modern leadership in this vibrant era of new thinking, realities and possibilities. D.A. provides a fresh perspective on how legendary leaders became so, and how new leaders have embraced core principles of leadership while shedding outdated models of execution and inventing their own methods using new tools and resources at their disposal.

As Chief Diversity & Inclusion Officer of the United States Tennis Association and a rising star in the organization for decades, D.A. has seen the power of leadership up close, from the emergence of exciting world-class athletes, to initiatives that have made the U.S. Open one of the most successful sporting events of all time.

As a social media expert and collaborative leader himself, D.A. Abrams can speak with authority about what it takes to lead in this competitive world.

As you read *New-School Leadership,* you'll learn ways to become and remain the most effective leader possible and how our ever-changing environment including technology, social media, global competition, and a diverse workplace, workforce, and marketplace will and should impact your leadership.

If you embrace the ideas in this book, you will become a better leader.

I promise.

**André Taylor**

Author, *You Can Still Win! Breakthrough Bounce Back, Come from Behind and Flourish,* and countless books, articles, audio, and video programs

Speaker, and celebrated leadership-development and management consultant

www.andretaylor.com

# ACKNOWLEDGEMENTS

I want to dedicate this book to Henry Talbert, my advisor, personal USTA consultant, and friend for over twenty years. He served as my leadership role model for decades and gave me, as he gave to so many others, my start at the United States Tennis Association.

When Henry passed away on January 12, 2014, American tennis lost an extraordinary individual. Gordon Smith, the USTA's Executive Director, described it best when he said, "Henry represented everything good about tennis and the USTA. He was in every sense the heart and soul of who we are and who we aspire to be."

I started playing tennis in the mid-70s, and around that time I first began to hear about the USTA's Henry Talbert. Similar to my feelings about Arthur Ashe, I viewed Mr. Talbert as an icon. He was the first African-American (and only, for a long time) to be a USTA administrator on the national level. In fact, Henry was a long-time member of the USTA's C-suite, long before the term was introduced.

I was very fortunate to become a member of Henry's Recreational Tennis Staff at the USTA in 1993. On my first day at the job, the highlight of my orientation was Henry's walking me through the USTA yearbook, page-by-page. I did not quite get it then, but soon came to understand and appreciate the benefit of this introduction to the Association and its history. In fact, this is something that I continue to do today with all new hires.

It did not take long for me to realize that having Henry as my boss was a very special experience. The following are just a few of his many attributes that had resounding impact on me:

1. Henry always (and I mean, *always*) began to articulate his thoughts by saying, "I have three

things." What's funny about it was, sometimes he would then make two points, or maybe even four, but he always began with, "I have three things." Sometimes I find myself using the same communications strategy today. *Three Things…*

2. As a member of Henry's team, you always knew that he had your back. Even when it wasn't in his best interest. I remember him covering for me on more than one occasion.

3. Henry was an ex-military man, so *rules* were very important to him. But, that said, his ***people*** were always more important than the rules.

4. Henry always led by example. He never asked his people to do things that he would not do. Today, we call this "walking the talk," but in his quiet way he didn't have to call it anything. This commitment continues to have impact on me.

5. Henry was a man of integrity. He always delivered on his promises, and he truly taught me the term, "Promise Less, Deliver More."

6. Henry's sense of humor was second to none. True, some of his jokes were bad, but when delivered by one Mr. Talbert, they were always funny, too.

7. Henry treated everyone with respect. I cannot remember a time when he reprimanded a subordinate publicly, including me. Sure, he reprimanded me privately a number of times, but never in a public or embarrassing way.

8. Henry was a man of high principle. He always provided his counsel in a respectful manner. This may be the most compelling reason why he was loved by representatives from so many facets of the tennis world.

9. Henry was a very hard and smart worker. I am convinced that he found a way to be of service to his mission fully seven days a week.

10. Henry never complained about his situation.


Henry Talbert was the very definition of class, a true gentleman, and one of the smartest as well as nicest people that I have had the pleasure of knowing. He continues to serve as my role model, at the USTA, as an exemplary husband and father, and as a leader of others. The life lessons that he taught me will always stand the test of time, and his legacy will live on through all of the people whom he touched.

# INTRODUCTION

Do you have a favorite business book? One that has caught your imagination, expanded your capacity, or helped you to improve some aspect of running your organization? I do. Many of them, in fact. Tony Hsieh's Delivering Happiness, Onward by Howard Schultz, Timothy Ferriss' *4-Hour Work Week.* Gary Vaynerchuck's *Jab Jab Jab Right Hook.* Michael Lewis' *Moneyball.* Lots of things by Seth Godin.

Or maybe you have been inspired by certain CEOs and top managers, people who have wisdom and grace, who are dynamic and successful, who seem to lead without effort and yet remain competitive and ahead of the curve? Steve Jobs *(Apple).* Ursula Burns *(Xerox).* Marissa Mayer *(Yahoo!).* Kenneth Chennault *(American Express).* Sheryl Sanberg *(Facebook).*

I find each one of these books and leaders to be educational; they regularly impact my own thinking and practice. Over the past twenty years, I have also been blessed to have had visionary mentors and to have worked with terrific leaders in my own positions at the USTA. These include the late Henry Talbert, Gordon Smith, Kurt Kamperman, Lee Hamilton, Pat Freebody, Rick Ferman, Bob Garry, and Marshall Happer, who have all helped me to formulate and effectuate my own thoughts on new-school leadership.

The one thing that I know to be true, no matter where you get your information, whom you follow, or what you study, is this: the needs for and demands on leadership have changed radically in the past few years. To be a dynamic and effective leader of a 21st-century organization or corporation requires an entirely different strategy and set of skills than it did just five or ten years ago. In fact, much of the best advice and examples from even the last decade *no longer apply.*

Your adjustment to the essential conditions of contemporary leadership begins with having a global mindset, of course. It requires an approach that embraces and accommodates the lightening-fast pace at which our companies, our customers, and our staff priorities are changing. It involves *seeing* and *setting* trends rather than *observing* and *following* them. And it demands a sophisticated and advanced style of communication that operates on many levels, directions, and platforms.

As AchieveGlobal discovered after doing a comprehensive leadership review in 2012, one which canvased much of the literature plus held focus groups and administered extensive surveys of global trends in leadership practices, *"Leadership in the 21ˢᵗ century is more than ever a **complex matrix of practices** ... Effective leaders recognize their own leadership strengths and liabilities, adjust current strategies, adopt new strategies, and recognize strengths and liabilities in other people. Leaders strong in the Reflection Zone are better equipped to leverage their strengths and reduce their liabilities."*[1]

This book is a summary from my own "Reflection Zone," and the product of my own implementation of best leadership practices in my professional life as Chief Diversity & Inclusion Officer for the United States Tennis Association. It springs from a widely-shared definition of effective new-school leaders by scholar and leadership-studies pioneer Warren Bennis that they are "those who innovate, originate, initiate, develop, focus on people, inspire trust, have a long-range view, ask what and why, have their eye on the horizon, and challenge the status quo."[2]

This book looks at fundamental ways to become and remain the most effective leader possible, given the current institutional and corporate landscape. It hopes to ensure that we have inspiring and visionary leaders at the heads of our organizations, divisions, and institutions. My thesis and new-school model pertain to leaders in the traditional areas of finance, business and politics, but also are at the core of inspirational leaders in the arenas of sports, non-profit associations, beauty, spiritual organizations and families, if not more.

"Leaders can arise in any or all areas of life," as best-selling author John Demartini reminds us.[3] My new-school leadership model applies to each one of them.

As Canadian entrepreneur and leadership analyst Matthew MacDonald summarizes it, "Leadership is influencing and motivating others to work towards an established goal that furthers their organization and/or movement. Where there is any strong leader, there is a group of followers willing to be led."[4]

At fundament is this core concept that leaders strike a vision and bring along a wide network of stakeholders in order to realize the strategic direction that will best serve their company or association. Now, more than ever, this is a very participatory process that has moved swiftly beyond the notion of sending down orders and watching them happen. New-school leaders recognize that, "no matter how you look at it, no matter which field you are in, no matter how brilliant your ideas are, success is a team sport."[5] As leaders, we have many people to move, and so, enhancing our personal effectiveness has become more important than ever before.

I recognize how complex it has become for us to be effective leaders for our associations and corporations. There are many books and talks that teach "about" leadership. Most organizations acknowledge the institutional benefits of the many courses and trainings that seek to improve productivity or increase leadership capabilities and performance.[6] But I have observed that there is much less support to be found around the idea of "how" to actually lead our companies and ourselves, given the latest conditions and demands.

I believe, through exploring and then enhancing the qualities encompassed by this new-school leadership model, you will feel empowered to do what is needed to lead success in your enterprise: to develop an inspiring vision for the future of your institutions, to then align your team members through effective communication about where you are headed as well as why and how, and then to engage and motivate each 21ˢᵗ-century customer, manager, and stakeholder in ways that deliver the impact and performance that your organization requires.

I have distilled my vision for a new-school leadership model into the following components:

**L = Lifelong Learner**

**E = Engagement**

**A = Ahead of the Curve**

**D = Diversity & Inclusion**

**E = Empathy**

**R = Relationship Management**

**S = Social Media Presence**

**H = High Energy**

**I = Influence & Enrollment**

**P = Platinum Rule**

I am convinced that these are what constitute a skilled, successful, and happy leader of any sort of business today: corporation, association, or organization; it applies to leadership in the for-profit, government, educational and NGO sectors, as well. Given the dynamic and progressive environment that we all face as leaders, I believe that we need to focus on those tenets in order to improve and solidify our leadership capacity. I go into the components of this model in depth, with this book. To these I add a core group of "must-have" attributes which ensure that a 21st-century leader makes the impact to which she or he aspires, in our swiftly-changing world. The "must-haves" are:

- ❖ **Vision**
- ❖ **Purpose**
- ❖ **Passion**
- ❖ **Good Communication Skills**
- ❖ **Management Ability**

Finally, I look into ways to apply this model to your own enterprise in order to gain the "unfair advantage" that we all seek, in order to dominate our sector or sphere.

I have been a leader myself now for many years, and I have also had the good fortune to have been led, guided, mentored, and taught by myriad excellent leaders, as well. To this day, however, one of my very best bosses and leaders was my first, Jim Albaugh at Control Data Corporation. He had a great deal of impact not just on my own leadership style, but on the philosophies and strategies that I share in this book.

Jim always put *people first,* before the work that we had at hand. Of course, the work needed to get done, but it was clear to all of us who worked for him that he cared about his staff. For example, when Jim's boss assigned him a task at 6:00 PM that needed to be completed by the end of the day, he stayed with his team for the four hours it took to deliver the project, helping us all out, and then he invited us all out to a very late dinner—on him! Not at the company's expense.

His entire staff was included at his 40th birthday party, and welcomed at his home along with personal friends and family. He included me on cross-country skiing adventures with his family and dinners at his home, while taking on a mentoring role in addition to being my boss. Even long after I stopped reporting to him, directly, he inspired my leadership ability by continuing to coach and support me, and informed my ideas on influence, enrollment, and management.

Jim always inspired me with his *clear expectations:* he was very good at ensuring that his team knew what was expected and how the work that we did would fit into the overall picture.

It was unique at the time to work *with us* to establish performance measures. He also made sure to meet each of his staff members more than required, in order to ensure that we were on track. If together we found that our work no longer made sense, we would re-adjust. He was always available to answer questions and provide guidance, and made every effort to ensure that there were no surprises. He had empathy, he modeled inclusiveness, and he communicated in an admirable way with each one of us who worked for him.

Jim was a *smart worker* and very dedicated. He looked out for his boss and his team, managing in both directions with intelligence and diplomacy. I took careful notice of his communication skills, particularly his capacity to listen well, which was exemplary. Because he understood the culture and policies of our organization, and shared his knowledge freely, he knew which issues to fight for and how to sell his ideas. He had lasting impact on me as how to become a great influencer. And he never stinted on the credit, praise, and rewards for good work and great performance to anyone throughout the organization.

He informed me a great deal on relationship management as a core capacity for a great leader. And even modeled the necessary acknowledgement that, when a team member does not share your vision or performs poorly on assignments, they needed to be transferred or dismissed in order for you to lead effectively and efficiently.

Finally, Jim Albaugh taught me by example how essential it is, as a leader, to excel not just in your domain, but to prioritize all manner of ***selling your ideas***: whether upwards, to your bosses; sideways, to your colleagues and stakeholders; as well as downwards to your subordinates within the organization. As I discuss more deeply throughout the book, **people do business with people whom they know, like, and trust.** Whenever I think of my first leader and former boss, Jim Albaugh, I think of this precept above all others.

In the chapters that follow, let me share with you what I have discovered, and the model that inspires me to lead well and with passion.

Whether it is Henry Talbert or Jeff Bezos, Jim Albaugh or Oprah Winfrey or your own best leader, whoever teaches and inspires *you* as they have *me*, they no doubt exemplify this new-school leadership model that I explore through the book, and it has contributed to their efficacy and success. It can do the same, for you.

# CHAPTER 1

# THAT WAS THEN/THIS IS NOW

*"Learning and innovation go hand in hand. The arrogance of success is to think that what you did yesterday will be sufficient for tomorrow."*

*—William Pollard*

While much is made of the evolution of leadership techniques and strategies over time, in my opinion we are observing a sea-change at this moment. Whether due to advances in technology or developments in human attitude, leadership has experienced an epistemological shift in the last 5-10 years. As a result, the essential skills and trends that will ensure the best results for our companies and associations are very different now than what we may have been taught, or than we might have relied upon in years past.[8]

As Holly Green, CEO and Managing Director of The Human Factor, Inc., summarizes so concisely in her *Forbes* blog, "Previous generations of leaders could at least count on a reasonably stable world, where change unfolded at a much slower pace. These days, the past is increasingly less predictive, the future is almost unimaginable, and the present exists for about a nano-second."[9] Where once we looked to our leaders to administrate and direct, we now require them to guide and inspire. Effective leaders in volatile times need vibrant visions that "cut through today's clutter of information to communicate (them) to multiple stakeholders in a memorable way."[10]

The transformation that is required by this radical shift ripples through every aspect of our business life. For example, as General Atlantic Chairman Steve Denning explains, "the Fortune 500 are becoming increasingly unproductive because they are run as hierarchical bureaucracies."[11] These mighty companies' whole vision of leadership and success is rapidly becoming outdated by a changing world. Let's look at where we've been, and the leadership strategies that I see as becoming swiftly less useful with each passing day. This will throw into stark relief the new circumstances that must be understood and embraced by new-school leadership.

# *Hallmarks of the Past*

The major characteristics of highly successful leadership in the past involved the "top-down" model of an authoritarian approach to running companies or organizations. Strict protocols and regulations accompanied precise orders by professional managers. Once a leader took a decision or direction, he or she then enlisted his or her managers to do *what* was wanted by prescribing *where* and *how* it was to be done, and *when* it needed to be accomplished.

Traditionally, problems were often solved by blaming and shaming. There was a "my way or the highway" mentality in many enterprises and institutions. A certain level of intimidation and right/wrong analysis were effective ways to kick-butt and get things moving in the right direction. And rarely was it the *leaders themselves* who took responsibility for their mistakes or impact on other members of the corporate community.

Many firms tended to look outward from the inside, with a sole priority of making the maximum profit for shareholders without regard for the unique needs of their customers. In addition, employees were often tired, bored, stressed, and unsatisfied. Statistically speaking about the employees at Fortune 500 companies, "only one in five is fully engaged in his or her work."[12] Instead of employee engagement, traditional corporate leaders have focused on lowering costs, improving their value chain, and "pushing their products and services at customers."[13]

Old-school governments and educational institutions have had leadership with outmoded priorities, as well. In addition, we are swiftly starting to see that the U.S. health-services bureaucracy can no longer sustain itself, either, if it continues to prioritize and accommodate only the vast network of insurance bureaucrats and administrators over the care and economic needs of its customers and patients.

The factory-based idea behind U.S. university leadership, which makes a priority out of increasing profits and "producing" more and more graduates with just higher grades, has also started to fade in response to the creative economy of the 21st century. The familiar test-driven education system's bureaucracy is clearly not preparing our students anymore for the swiftly-changing job market in which they find themselves after they leave school.[14]

It's been said that old-school organizations were perfectly well designed to obtain the results that they achieved. So, if our leaders and their organizations maintain any aspects of that traditional course, they are destined to produce the very same things. Today, however, we need <u>new</u> results in order to keep up with the more connected world in which we find ourselves.[15]

*Success* in any and every sector that you can name already means something altogether different.

New models of leadership for attracting stakeholders, for training staff, and for organizing our institutions now have to meet the realities of today, and the challenges of tomorrow. Everything is different now, including how we lead!

## What does "Today" Look Like?

Today's management landscape is complex. Our employees span multiple generations, cultures, and backgrounds; they have very different styles, interests, and needs, not all of which are compatible with one another! Our marketplaces are highly competitive, expectations are high, loyalty is fleeting, and customer attraction and retention is very different than it once was.

In fact, you could say that there really is no longer a conventional "manager" environment at all. "Today's employees want to be led. They want to participate and engage in every aspect of their job."[16] This is exciting, actually, when you're a leader. The opportunities are ripe for development and success. But they now demand a much more participatory style of leadership, and consistent two-way channels of communication, in order to succeed.

We have already touched on this radical shift in the speed of life that we have all experienced, and which comprises any corporate or association environment today. Competition is now in real time. Decisions must be made swiftly and in spite of uncertainty. And leaders must now be able to "see and appreciate the big picture ... understand how the different parts of their enterprise work."[17] They can't just focus on "their" silo or sector, not if they hope to be an effective leader today.

The authoritarian style has been replaced by a participative one. The "group" has become central to any enterprise or endeavor. Leaders just don't make decisions alone anymore, at least not optimum ones. Our most successful and innovative institutions now incorporate flex-time and flexible workscapes that encourage collaboration; leaders and managers incorporate much more two-way communication with employees and customers in their decision-making, rather than rely on old-school models of orders and directives.

This mode of leadership has become critical in part because, "in general, people do not like to have ideas or solutions imposed on them."[18] New-school leadership skills involve inspiring and engaging followers without mandating or ordering. What has become critical to the effectiveness of leaders today is to achieve a concrete, participatory "buy-in" from everyone involved in a decision, direction, or departure. What has evolved, in order to adapt to the changing nature of employees and stakeholders, is that leaders today "believe that their group members have definite value to add" and "ensure that there is a genuine desire for each team member's input into the outcome."[19] In fact, today's staff can tell on a deep level whether or not their leaders want and appreciate their personal commitments to more than just the bottom line.

If you are evolving your leadership identity to lead a new generation of employees, you will have noticed that some aspects of the new episteme that leaders must embrace today are indeed due to a generational change. Baby Boomers are retiring; the Gen X and Millennial employees and managers in our workforce have different priorities and styles than their predecessors. Statistically significant as well is the fact that, both in the U.S. and worldwide, there is a 20% smaller talent pool of managers rising from these two generations, so not only is skilled leadership required to manage a multi-generational enterprise, but also careful attention needs to be paid in order to attract and retain the very best of this emerging talent pool. New-school leaders are either leading this workforce or they *are* Gen X members.[20]

You will find that new-school workers have been encouraged to collaborate and value teamwork, rather than to follow someone just because they're in charge; they prefer to assume autonomy rather than endure micro-management. They want enough time for their personal lives and choose less rigid, more fun corporate cultures. They thrive under a new generation of leaders who value "action, so they (too) work more efficiently and productively to earn time off."[21] And they follow leaders who have heart.

New-school leaders themselves are required to be more self-aware than ever before. Effective and inspiring leadership involves copping to missteps or poor direction, and making amends or course corrections within full view of employees and stakeholders. Our very best leaders today are candid, they listen well, and they have become highly attuned to everything around them, both within their institutions and outside. Their lines of communication have expanded vastly beyond just their direct reports and stockholders. They know that our world becomes smaller on a daily basis, and hence that diversity and inclusion are key components of their institutional success.

Today's new-school leaders are, as General Atlantic Chairman Steve Denning summarizes, "focused on looking from the outside-in, understanding the many varieties of people with whom they might do business, comprehending their hopes and dreams, their problems and goals, and trying to find ways to delight them. Rather than 'pushing' products and services at customers, they are deploying the power of 'pull.' They must recognize that we are living in the age of customer capitalism."[22]

Due to the speed and complexity of today's business environment, plus this heightened awareness along with greatly expanded channels of communication, leaders are now oftentimes required to juggle very mixed messages and conflicting information. New-school leadership today involves parsing a whole new and wider set of inputs than it once did.[23]

What is the ideal model to lead and transform such a dynamic but confusing and challenging world that clearly *is* our new reality?

## *And Whatever It Is, It's Changing!*

As the Dale Carnegie Institute reminds us, "Organizations today operate in an environment of rapid, continuous change. Significant internal changes include reorganizations, retirements, and hiring, external changes include shifts in the marketplace, evolving expectations of clients, and innovation. Leading a changing organization is a demanding, time-consuming responsibility."[24]

The key responsibility of a leader at any point in history has been to cope with *change.* New-school leaders take responsibility for the well-being of their institutions, their employees, their clients and customers, and their communities, as well, in a rapidly evolving and technologically advancing world.

In my experience, leading change is likely one of the biggest challenges we face, and so all of the tenets of the new-school leadership model that you will find described throughout this book are designed to make us the best change-leaders possible.

As we accept and embrace the components of our hyper-changing world, there is a foundation of leadership that prepares us to be successful, stabile, and transformative for our organizations and corporations. The following chapter looks at the components of new-school leadership that prepare you for today *and* tomorrow.

### CONTRAST BETWEEN OLD STYLE LEADERSHIP & THE NEW, EMERGING MOVEMENTAL INFLUENCE

| | | |
|---|---|---|
| **Measure of Influence:** | Numbers of people hearing | Numbers of people being heard |
| **Leader's Role:** | Guardian of a vision | Empower others to discover their vision |
| **Authority:** | Delegated from the top | Distributed out toward the margins |
| **Goal:** | Entertain a larger audience | Equip a select army of people |
| **Leader's value:** | Needed for organization's success | Not necessary for organization's success |
| **Means:** | Gathering as many as possible | Targeting smaller influential groups |
| **Mechanism:** | Teaching in an inspiring event | Training people to teach in multiple contexts |
| **Context:** | The meeting place | The market place |
| **Growth Aims:** | Fast/large start: Addition | Slow/small start that builds: Multiplication |
| **Growth means:** | Organizational (Better programming in the event/product) | Organic (Better DNA in everyone) |
| **Legacy:** | A monument | A movement |
| **Style:** | Complex specialty: More is better | Profound via simplicity: Less is more |
| **Pool of leaders:** | The ordained few | The ordinary masses |
| **Cost:** | Expensive | Potentially Free |
| **Income:** | Can make lots of money | Will not generate revenue |
| **Organization:** | Control to maintain order & outcome | Order without control of outcome |
| **Results:** | Dependence | Empowerment |

*Neil Cole © 2012–Used with permission*[25]

# Leadership Spotlight

"Let us not forget that *the leaders of civil society represent the long view; they're the people who lay the foundation for lasting progress.* In our own country, theirs is the type of commitment that ended slavery, enabled women's suffrage, brought the dream of civil rights closer to reality, improved workplace safety, and reduced the pollution of water and air.

"On the global stage, in just the past few decades, civil society has helped to end apartheid, extend democracy on every continent, fight back against human trafficking, raise awareness about global warming, and curb the trade in dirty diamonds."[26]

—*Samantha Power, American academic, author and diplomat who currently serves as the United States Ambassador to the United Nations. A former Executive Director of the Carr Center for Human Rights Policy at Harvard University's Kennedy School of Government, she assumed office in August 2013*

# CHAPTER 2

# NEW-SCHOOL LEADERSHIP MODEL

*"If your actions inspire others to dream more, learn more, do more, and become more, you are a leader."*
—**John Quincy Adams**

FedEx founder and CEO Fred Smith once said, "In business, the big thing is making sure the big thing *stays* the big thing."[27] The Big Thing in new-school leadership is how to create a vision, bring that vision alive, and do it with the right people who have all been inspired to follow you on the path that will generate success.

This chapter outlines my 10-part leadership model that identifies the critical components of a new-school leader. Each aspect can be cultivated and practiced as a way of making us more successful and satisfied in our pursuit of leading great organizations and corporations.

## L = Lifelong Learner

*The most dangerous leadership myth is that leaders are born-that there is a genetic factor to leadership. That's nonsense; in fact, the opposite is true. Leaders are made rather than born.*

—*Warren Bennis*

Every great leader today is curious and committed to the constant pursuit of new knowledge, skills, and understanding. Many leaders have terrific educations, and/or are mentored by the best, in their rise to the top of their associations or business entities. But there is still no end to the wisdom about psychology and human nature that we can study and absorb, information about developments in technology and communication that we need to keep abreast of, and the inspiration that can be drawn from success stories around us, not to mention the perceptive insights that can be gleaned from our employees, our customers, our kids, and all of the other stakeholders of our enterprise.

What makes **lifelong learning** a top component of new-school leadership is the starkly apparent fact that virtually no occupations or industries remain the same over time, any longer. So not only does each job need to be updated and learned, but so does the holistic comprehension of leaders who lead employees performing those jobs.[28]

New-school leaders have an internal drive to improve themselves constantly. I do not have a prescription for the ideal platforms or pathways through which a leader should continue their learning. But it is very clear that a new-school leader makes this a consistent and steady practice throughout his or her career.

I also support the idea of **pervasive learning** that Dan Pontefract describes in his book *Flat Army,* about "learning at the speed of need,"[29] and how it is impossible for a leader to "know" everything about a subject anymore, but that she is totally capable of knowing where to find critical information on any topic, when the need arises.[30] The other component of **pervasive learning** is that we have now done away with the idea of "training as an event," which is a fixed, closed-end mindset; the new-school leader replaces that with, as Pontrefact summarizes it, "learning (as) a collaborative, continuous, connected and community-based" growth mindset.

Furthermore, I believe that new-school leaders should expect continuous learning and self-improvement "from every person at every level of (your) organization."[31] So, part of a great leader's responsibility is to find ways to inspire your employees to continue their learning and skills development, both for their personal satisfaction and capacity, but also so that they remain constant sources of innovation and new ideas that can be brought to you and your company.[32]

# E = Engagement

*As we look ahead into the next century, leaders will be those who empower others.*

—Bill Gates

Here is a statistic that I found dramatic and, frankly, a bit shocking: Only 13% of employees worldwide are engaged at work, according to Gallup's new 142-country study on the *State of the Global Workplace*. This translates to the fact that only about one in every eight workers studied around the world was "psychologically committed to their jobs and likely to be making positive contributions to their organizations."[33]

Of the remaining 87% of employees worldwide, "63% are 'not engaged,' meaning they lack motivation and are less likely to invest discretionary effort in organizational goals or outcomes. And 24% are 'actively disengaged,' indicating they are unhappy and unproductive at work and liable to spread negativity to coworkers. In rough numbers, this translates into 900 million not engaged and 340 million actively disengaged workers around the globe."[34]

This is a monumental challenge for corporate and organizational leaders. Imagine the effectiveness of our associations and institutions if those numbers regarding our employees' support and enthusiasm were reversed?!

New-school leaders make engagement a top priority. As best-selling author Peter Economy (*Managing for Dummies, The Management Bible, Leading through Uncertainty)* reminds us, "Every employee is a source of unlimited ideas on how to improve his or her organization's products, work processes, and systems. Most employees simply need to be invited to participate and then positively reinforced when they do."[35] Mr. Economy adds this critical rejoinder, however: "employee participation only works in an environment of complete and unconditional trust."[36]

That is where new-school leadership in the area of **employee engagement** comes in. Excellent leaders commit time and resources to inspiring engagement, setting engagement standards and benchmarks, and measuring their progress in institutions large and small.

For smaller workplaces, you may not need to do broad polling in order to assess your employee engagement effectively. One-on-one meetings with employees might do the trick. At medium and larger workplaces, you may want to supplement those with town hall meetings, for example, or annual surveys and/or internal focus groups. A strategy that has been shown to provide leaders with the most reliable, successful data about their engagement is to ask all of their employees, whatever their level or department, the same questions on a regular basis. This permits leaders to best analyze the feedback they receive, and then to design more targeted action steps, as a consequence.

One reliable basic instrument is Gallup's "G12 feedback system," based on the factors that determine both active engagement and disengagement for most workers. Their research (which consistently shows a correlation between high survey scores and superior job performance) developed this series of questions, which are rated on a scale from 1-5:

1. Do I know what is expected of me at work?
2. Do I have the materials and equipment that I need in order to do my work right?
3. At work, do I have the opportunity to do what I do best every day?
4. In the last seven days, have I received recognition or praise for doing good work?
5. Does my supervisor, or someone at work, seem to care about me as a person?
6. Is there someone at work who encourages my development?
7. At work, do my opinions seem to count?
8. Does the mission or purpose of my company make me feel that my job is important?
9. Are my coworkers committed to doing quality work?
10. Do I have a best friend at work?
11. In the past six months, has someone at work talked to me about my progress?
12. This past year, have I had opportunities at work to learn and grow?[37]

Quantum Workplace is another leader in building science-based tools to measure and manage employee engagement, loyalty and retention. They have slightly different survey questions for assessing engagement, which ask that the following statements be ranked on a scale of 1 to 10[38]:

1. Management provides good leadership and guidance during difficult economic conditions.

2. My job is mentally stimulating.

3. I understand how my work contributes to my company's performance.

4. There are future opportunities for growth at my company.

5. My company affords me the opportunity to develop my skills.

6. I receive recognition and reward for my contributions.

7. There is open, honest communication between employees and managers.

8. I see professional growth and career opportunities for myself in this organization.

9. I know how I fit into the organization's future plans.

10. Considering the value I bring to the organization, I am paid fairly.

I emphasize this component of new-school leadership because engagement has a direct impact on corporate success, stability, and economic growth. And engaged employees are more productive! They have better attendance records, and longer-term loyalty to remain with their companies once trained and enmeshed within your corporate structure. Stanford University Graduate School Business (GSB) professor Robert Sutton said in a recent interview that "you want people with a sense of accountability, who feel like 'I own the place, and the place owns me.' They will push themselves and each other, feel obligated to teach and to learn."[39]

As Gallup workplace researcher Sangeeta Agrawal reports, "When people are more engaged, their companies do better, and those companies have room to add more people. When employees are not engaged or are actively disengaged, their companies don't do as well, they don't hire new workers, and they may even lay off the workers they have. But when the ratio between engaged employees and actively disengaged employees improves, the whole company improves. That, in turn, can improve whole economies."[40]

New-school leaders have an opportunity to have impact not just within their associations or companies, through improving and refining their employee engagement, but even in the wider economy. As Jennifer Robison and Steve Crabtree reported in *Gallup Business Journal*, "Engaged workplaces are most likely to be engines of job creation around the world. This insight is crucial to businesses, communities, and countries affected by the recession."[41]

Finally, recognize that **direct human interaction** is actually a "key differentiator that drives engagement and positive word of mouth."[42] We sometimes allow technology to stand in the stead of human interaction, whether it is through messaging, survey, reporting, or marketing. But when new-school leaders implement their overall engagement strategy, and look to improve their employees' involvement with them and their companies, they remember the human component of influencing these improvements.

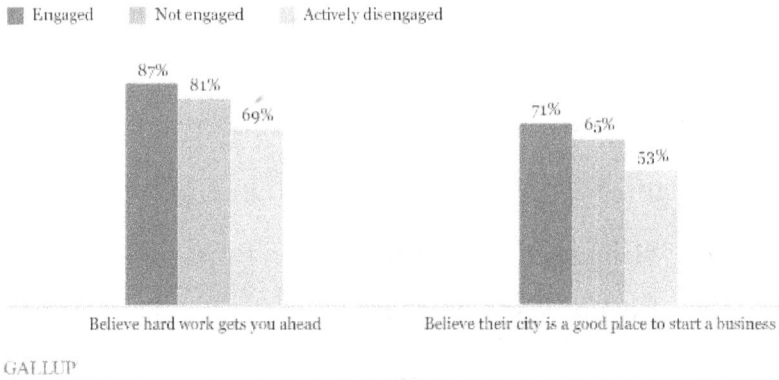

*Engaged Employees Boost Entrepreneurs' Confidence Worldwide*

Job creation depends on the confidence of entrepreneurs to start new ventures -- and engaged employees give that confidence a boost. Gallup data indicate that engaged employees not only make their own employers more successful through their hard work, but they also foster entrepreneurship in their communities. About seven in 10 engaged employees (71%) report that their city is a good place to start a business, compared with 53% of those who are actively disengaged.

■ Engaged    ■ Not engaged    ■ Actively disengaged

87%
81%
69%

71%
65%
53%

Believe hard work gets you ahead      Believe their city is a good place to start a business

GALLUP

*"State of the Global Workplace," Gallup 2013*

# A = Ahead of the Curve

***A leader takes people where they want to go. A great leader takes people where they don't necessarily want to go, but ought to be.***

—Rosalynn Carter

Since one of the core responsibilities of any leader is to lead change, and since change is not just a given within marketplaces and companies today, but is happening at break-neck speed, the new-school leader makes it a priority to remain **ahead of the curve.** Part of the **life-long learning** effort of successful leaders is to stay attuned to evolving trends. Their leadership vision and implementation must involve planning for and adapting to those social, technological, and economic developments that directly impact their corporation and stakeholders, or that *may* do so, in the very near future.[43]

The direct consequence of the communication and technology advances that have become the norm in our personal and business lives is not only the volume of data and complexity of relationships that barrage us daily: it's also that the world has become smaller, and our ability to serve and interact with ever-expanding communities continues to grow. That is an exciting set of opportunities for the new-school leader. But it also compels us to be "more innovative and proactive, anticipating problems and opportunities as well as entirely new markets and products"[44]

New-school leaders must remain in a position to observe the directions and consequences of trends, both on the ground and at a macro-level (and everywhere in between, of course!). They need to be able to synthesize input from many sources, whether it is through employees or clients, online or at home, in networking groups or about competitors, and then stay open to a flexible, swift adjustment of their strategies and response. New-school leaders who stay ahead of the curve are nimble, and they build their organizations in such a way that everyone can respond to trends. It is particularly critical to "foster an environment in which people have the power to change course quickly if a project or initiative isn't working."[45]

# D = Diversity & Inclusion

I believe that most savvy executives today are attuned already to the diversity of the contemporary U.S. marketplace, a reality which I call the "New Normal," and that I delineate extensively in my book *Diversity & Inclusion: The Big Six Strategy for Success*. That said, a recent comprehensive global leadership survey shows that while leaders of diverse organizations do value this component of leadership and corporate strategy somewhat, nevertheless, "leaders worldwide rank diversity of lowest importance among all leadership zones."[46] This is a grave mistake.

Every new-school leader needs two things: a full understanding of the diverse make-up of the full complement of their stakeholders and potential clients; and a comprehensive **diversity & inclusion** business strategy that builds not just their company, but its profit and influence, going forward.

The demographic reality of the U.S. is this: by 2016, 70% percent of the U.S. work force will be women and/or Black and Latino.[47] And how about those customers? Every leader's marketplace is being defined by the fact that, for the first time in U.S. history, less than half of all newborns in America are non-Hispanic Caucasian. The percentage of Americans who are white (non-Hispanic) is on a demographic trend downwards, particularly among our younger citizens. By 2050, according to the U.S. Census data, people of color will constitute the majority of our population.[48] This demographic shift is already showing its impact on our politics and economy.

So, as you can imagine, anyone who fails to fully embrace the "New Normal" of these changing demographics will also fail to capitalize on the substantial growth in buying power that these diverse markets represent. Not only are these diverse minority groups increasing as a percentage of the U.S. population, but so too is the buying power that they wield.

We are witnessing a "demographic tsunami" on other fronts as well, which will also impact the new-school leader's **diversity & inclusion plan.** For example, "millennials make up 36% of the 2014 U.S. workforce, and become almost half by 2020. Boomers are retiring at record numbers. For the first time a generation is entering the workforce engaged in technology well beyond what their employers use today."[49] This fact, too, redefines how a new-school leader leads change.

Also, despite the under-index of women in top management positions at either Fortune 500 companies or entrepreneur-led start-ups, Stanford Graduate School of Business Professor Robert Sutton reminds us in his new book, *Scaling Up Excellence,* "that you should make sure to have as many women as possible, because the more men you have in a group, the dumber it gets, controlling for their IQ. There's actually very good evidence of that."[50]

It has never been more critical for a leader to develop a comprehensive and holistic business approach to diversity & inclusion within their association or corporation. The goals of your D&I plan are to ensure a diverse workforce at every level, to reach a multi-cultural marketplace, and to include diversity in your company's image as a way to take advantage of the greatest opportunities for growth and expansion.

Ultimately, diversity and inclusion become part of a new-school leader's competitive advantage. I believe that D&I should be a cornerstone to any vision for achieving organizational or corporate goals and objectives. In my experience, there are few strategies that bolster a leader's bottom line in a more significant or enduring way.

# *Leadership Spotlight*

"Diversity and inclusion … is the core of our work, and it's important to say that progress has been made yet there is so much more work to do. We know that the foundation leaders do not reflect the diversity of this country and the browning of America over the next several years will widen this gap. Many foundations want to support vulnerable communities; communities of color disproportionately suffer poor outcomes and available data suggests that communities of color are underfunded and a few foundations actually identified communities of color as a focus in their missions or grant-making guidelines."[51]

—*Susan Taylor Batten, President and CEO of the Association of Black Foundation Executives (ABFE, which just celebrated 40 years of promoting effective and responsive philanthropy in Black communities.*

# *E = Empathy*

Jet Blue Airways Chairman Joel Peterson lectures at the Stanford GSB, and is known to remind young entrepreneurs and future leaders that "You catch more flies with honey." This is not new news, but his students are well aware that some schools of management still encourage leaders to "set a high bar and withhold praise, or to motivate by fear."[52]

Those who ascribe more to Peterson's approach cultivate **empathy** in their new-school leadership, and attune themselves emotionally to the psychological experiences of others. They lead with their hearts open to the needs and lives of those around them.

Of course, we all view the world and our institutions through a lens determined by our unique set of life experiences and knowledge. But we must be very cognizant of ways to expand our consciousness, when leading others in the 21$^{st}$ century. To begin with, a new-school leader's commitment to D&I invariably helps him or her to be exposed to and then embrace others' views and approaches.

From this vantage of expanded understanding of the myriad perspectives in a leader's personal and professional landscape, accompanied by a genuine interest in and concern for the circumstances of those around her, a leader can begin any action or negotiation from a place of cooperation and compromise. "By accepting the concept that we can all learn from each other, we can start to understand how to turn personality differences into positive business results."[53]

Empathy is a part of the new-school leadership model that needs particular attention because psychological research trends show many ways that the power that accompanies leadership can specifically diminish many varieties of empathy. "Power takes a bit out of that ability ... to adapt our behaviors to the behaviors of other people," says UC Berkeley social psychologist Dacher Keltner.[54] Keltner goes on to write about a new research field that is showing the ways in which leaders with power can develop their compassionate selves through coaching and practice. This is a valuable undertaking for all leaders, these days.

Peter Economy (*The Management Bible, Leading Through Uncertainty*) writes, "When you lead with your heart, others are sure to be touched, both inside and outside the organization. Putting people first is the key to unleashing the full power and creativity of employee teams, superior customer service, strengthened client relations, and closer and more productive relationships with vendors and suppliers."[55] When you act with empathy, it inspires an environment where support and praise flourish within your corporate culture.

Much has been written in recent years about emotional intelligence (EI); some HR and recruitment efforts even test for it now in prospective employees, as it is considered another trait of effective new-school leaders. It involves not just empathy and understanding others' emotions, but a capacity for controlling one's own.

The great thing about empathy and EI is that they are not fixed traits: they can all be *learned and practiced.*

The results are invariably positive, both on a leader's life and business, but also on those of their employees and teams.[56] Since leaders who appreciate their colleagues' and employees' emotions excel at results and success in their workplace, I rank empathy as a critical component of the new-school leader.

The additional caution for those of us living complicated, multi-screen, swiftly-paced lives, however, is this: research results build daily that show how *distraction* has a deleterious neurological impact on that part of our brain that responds emotionally to other people's psychological experiences.

As novelist Jonathan Safran Foer (*Everything is Illuminated*) summarized recently in *The New York Times,* "Psychologists who study empathy and compassion are finding that unlike our almost instantaneous responses to physical pain, it takes time for the brain to comprehend the psychological and moral dimensions of a situation. The more distracted we become, and the more emphasis we place on speed at the expense of depth, the less likely and able we are to care."[57]

Stanford Professor Clifford Nass (*The Man Who Lied to His Laptop: What Machines Teach Us About Human Relationships*) lays this problematic component of our ever-more distracted environment right at the feet of our technology. He thinks that "the ultimate risk of heavy technology use is that it diminishes empathy by limiting how much people engage with one another, even in the same room.

"'The way we become more human is by paying attention to each other,' he said. 'It shows how much you care.'

"That empathy, Mr. Nass said, is essential to the human condition. 'We are at an inflection point," he said. 'A significant fraction of people's experiences are now fragmented.'"[58]

The online habits that we have all ramped up as modern leaders are not just distracting us to the point that they affect our ability to think clearly. They are also having "negative effects on our emotional selves."

According to University of Southern California's Brain and Creativity Institute director Antonio Damasio, "higher emotions like empathy emerge from neural processes that are characterised by how slowly they emerge. ... *the more distracted we become, the less able we are to experience the subtlest, most distinctively human forms of empathy, compassion, and other emotions.*"[59]

New-school leaders need to be mindful of the forces working against their practice of empathy. Distractedness and multi-tasking are the latest factors to make imprints on our brain that require our conscious counteraction through mindfulness and active attention. As Nicholas Carr writes in his influential book *The Shallows,* "to get inside other people's emotional states requires calmness and, crucially, time and reflection."[60]

Leadership training specialist Bruna Martinuzzi has wondered about the best ways to teach and reinforce empathy, as it is such an important element for a leader's building of trust and deep relationship bonds. She considers empathy "an emotional and thinking muscle that becomes stronger the more we use it," and offers these practical tips to develop your own capacity for empathy:

1. *Listen–truly listen to people. Listen with your ears, eyes and heart. Pay attention to others' body language, to their tone of voice, to the hidden emotions behind what they are saying to you, and to the context.*

2. *Don't interrupt people. Don't dismiss their concerns offhand. Don't rush to give advice. Don't change the subject. Allow people their moment.*

3. *Tune in to non-verbal communication. This is the way that people often communicate what they think or feel, even when their verbal communication says something quite different.*

4. *Practice the "93-percent rule". We know from a famous study by Professor Emeritus, Albert Mehrabian of UCLA, when communicating about feelings and attitudes, words–the things*

*we say—account for only 7 percent of the total message that people receive. The other 93% percent of the message that we communicate when we speak is contained in our tone of voice and body language. It's important, then, to spend some time to understand how we come across when we communicate with others about our feelings and attitudes.*

5. *Use people's name. Also remember the names of people's spouse and children so that you can refer to them by name.*

6. *Be fully present when you are with people. Don't check your email, look at your watch or take phone calls when a direct report drops into your office to talk to you. Put yourself in their shoes. How would you feel if your boss did that to you?*

7. *Smile at people.*

8. *Encourage people, particularly the quiet ones, when they speak up in meetings. A simple thing like an attentive nod can boost people's confidence.*

9. *Give genuine recognition and praise. Pay attention to what people are doing and catch them doing the right things. When you give praise, spend a little effort to make your genuine words memorable: "You are an asset to this team because..."; "This was pure genius"; "I would have missed this if you hadn't picked it up."*

10. *Take a personal interest in people. Show people that you care, and genuine curiosity about their lives. Ask them questions about their hobbies, their challenges, their families, their aspirations.*[61]

# R = Relationship Management

*A great person attracts great people and knows how to hold them together.*

—Johann Wolfgang Von Goethe

We all know that business is built on relationships, and that profitable, enduring businesses rely on a network of strong relationships in order to remain successful. The new-school leadership model looks at the changing nature of managing relationships both on the inside of a company or organization and on the outside, and identifies concrete strategies for ensuring that critical relationships grow deeper and more mutually beneficial to all parties involved.

The new-school leader's business, like her or his personal life, depends on other people, both for its profitability as well as for the impact of its services or products. Time and again it has been shown that a person's ability to build equitable relationships is directly related to their effectiveness in business. So, excellent leadership demands that both thought and effort be put into **forging strong, rich relationships** on all fronts: clients and customers, colleagues and peers, distributors and suppliers, co-workers and employees, boards of directors and service providers, community leaders and competitors.[62]

The building and management of a new-school leader's relationships involves forthright and excellent communication, which are skills that I discuss in depth in later sections, too. We mentioned already that *dialogue* rather than mandates, *empathic listening*, and an *openness* to information and input from all levels of a leader's professional and personal life are part of the ideal and critical new-school communication strategies. As Peter Economy (*Managing for Dummies, The Management Bible*) reiterates, "the best leaders encourage an open flow of ideas throughout the organization, and break down the walls that separate employees from one another."[63] This is the foundation of excellent relationships.

Leaders are constantly guiding and inspiring a group of followers, whether it's investors or employees, buyers or colleagues; usually, it's all of the above. They are establishing goals for their organization or association, and using their influence to enlist the support and cooperation of every stakeholder within their sphere. Each of these relationships is established, built, and then maintained for the betterment of the business and for the capacity of the leader.[64]

New-school leaders start by identifying and establishing those very best and specific high-quality relationships that will deliver on their mission. It may sound simple that a leader needs to put the right people into the right places within their companies, but, as Oracle President Mark V. Hurd says, "business leaders of today have to be able to master this ... indispensable discipline ... and be able to build management teams that truly understand the big picture, that understand how their teams must engage inside and outside the company to deliver maximum value, and stay laser-focused on making that strategy come fully alive for customers and prospects."[65]

New-school leaders hire well, and then they also know how to cultivate and grow strong relationships by learning first about the needs of each other party. In most initial interactions between two people who are negotiating a burgeoning relationship, there is generally some degree of hope or optimism mitigated by caution or concern. Two people rarely agree on *everything,* so, as relationships start, there is a period of learning and appraisal. New-school leaders find success by drawing attention **toward** new partners at the outset, and **away** from themselves, as a way of being inclusive. They know that all good relationships take **time**, so they also permit their successful ones to grow through patience and mutual experience, putting respect at the center of their appraisals and interactions.[66]

Any connection that grows into a valued working relationship is bound to benefit both parties, so new-school leaders know that they are investing in something which will redound to them eventually. They do not necessarily look for the fruits of their partnership up front, however.

Relationship management also involves the negotiation of power struggles that leaders often encounter within their high-test management teams. A new-school leader recognizes that these sorts of contentious or competitive relationships inside of their organization wastes valuable energy, resources and social currency, so he or she doesn't ignore them.

As I mentioned earlier, the new-school model draws from a more egalitarian leadership philosophy, and research published in *The Journal of Applied Psychology* has shown that, when applied directly to management, it diffuses power struggles and enhances clarity. When new-school relationships are tended in such a way that a leader's team members are all on the same page about peoples' leadership and power, from top leaders to managers to staff, their productivity and efficiency are greatly enhanced.[67]

There are distinct differences between the relationships that leaders have with members of the various and different generations that are represented in a contemporary workplace, notably between Baby

Boomers, Gen Xers and Millennials, since the younger leaders work so differently. Hence, part of new-school relationship management always bears these distinctions in mind.

New generations of workers have a different relationship to their companies and work life in general, so they will have a different relationship to leadership. They have observed in their parents' experiences the ways in which work-related burnout generally lowers quality of life, and they have noticed the lack of loyalty that companies demonstrated towards Baby Boomer workers over the last twenty years. As a result, workers and leaders aged 22-46 are defining a different relationship to how they earn a living, including telecommuting, continual training for professional evolution, and flexible hours. They aren't impressed by the idea that a job is something that you hate, or that you're "paying your requisite dues" through professional suffering and tough, dull work. These are not things that they value or tolerate well.

They know how to be more efficient through technology, and they don't look to leaders or managers to supervise progress too closely. Their relationships are very much grounded in the teamwork model, and they invest a great deal in collegial relationships. They do respond to feedback, but they are looking at leadership and management structures generally more as a "lattice" than in terms of the long-familiar corporate "ladder."[68] New-school leaders manage their workplace relationships by enmeshing with their employees and by appreciating the priorities and feedback of their multi-generational team members.

In addition, now more than ever, a new-school leader develops new strategies for managing customer relationships, as well. Microsoft New Zealand CRM Manager Paul Bowkett tells a story about renting a small formal bowtie from a local shop, and noting how impressed he was by his positive customer experience, even more so than by the item he wanted or its favorable price. When the store then sent him a personal thank-you email and invitation to discounts made available through their Facebook page, he became a bona fide loyal fan of the place.

As he writes, "the timing and tone of the email and the effort that went into building that connection left a lasting impression, ensuring I will go back and continue to deal with them."[69]

As you develop your own new-school leadership practice, remember that relationship management also involves input in and investment between your company and its market or clients. Microsoft's Pual Bowkett offers these ideas to remember when thinking of customer retention from a relationship perspective:

- ✓ *Regular, relevant and timely communication*
- ✓ *Give loyal customers preferential treatment*
- ✓ *Move from a transaction-based relationship to a partnership*
- ✓ *Don't try to move things too fast*
- ✓ *Be open and authentic*[70]

# S = *Social Media Presence*

No one's life is untouched by social media these days. New-school leaders, however, know how to harness its potential as a way to realize their vision. They maximize social media tools in order to build their personal and corporate brands, and use them to support their two-way communication and relationship management with staff, customers, markets, stakeholders, and future or potential communities.

Social media covers a spectrum of online sites, applications, and services. New-school leaders cultivate their presence in professional areas like LinkedIn, as well as on interactive platforms like Twitter. They know, for themselves and for their companies, projects, or programs, that Facebook is more than a place to share family anecdotes, and that Google+, Pinterest and Instagram can be easy ways to build and expand select networks.

As Duke Adjunct Business Professor Dorie Clark wrote in the *Harvard Business Review*, "If your digital footprint is lacking and you don't have a presence on basic sites like LinkedIn or Twitter, you're likely to be dismissed as a *Luddite*. Indeed, even the basic notion of writing a resume is becoming antiquated; your 'shadow resume' is Google."[71] New-school leaders are very savvy about being sure that their profiles are consistent, positive, and reflect well on themselves and their enterprises. They keep their information current, but don't overexpose themselves on multiple sites or pages.

Social media has already had significant impact on our employees and our customers; new-school leaders are cognizant of the salient developments in social media trending and their impact. For example, as studies begin to show that our brains are being rewired by technology and the regular use of social media, researchers are discovering that our attention spans have shortened. Most people are engaged with mobile messages virtually *all* of the time, but not with any one thing for long. So "fast and bite-sized" are the drivers of new-school messaging; social media savvy eschews long emails and lengthy presentations.

*Twitter*, for example, has become of potent tool in recent years, and often serves the new-school leader who seeks to listen and communicate broadly through short, frequent bursts of information rather than in longer blog formats. The advantage of this platform is the opportunity for a leader to appear "authentic," and to use social media in a way that increases access to and for her. While some leaders don't see the business case for posting or retweeting messages, former Medtronic CEO Bill George (now a professor at the Harvard Business School), says, "People want CEOs who are real. They want to know what you think," adding: "Can you think of a more cost-effective way of getting to your customers and employees?"[72]

While seven in ten Fortune 500 CEOs had no presence on the major social networks, as noted recently by CEO.com's *2013 Social CEO Report,* even the percentage of those who do is strikingly low: 4% have Twitter accounts under their name, and 8% are on Facebook. (This compares with 34% of Americans who are on Twitter, and 50% who use Facebook in the same time period.)[73] Those CEOs who do dive in, however, saw an average growth of 68.8 followers per day in 2013. People want to know what new-school leaders have to say!

CEOs from Aetna (Mark Bertolini) to Yahoo! (Melissa Mayer) to the highly-popular Warren Buffett (whose number of followers grew at a rate of over 800 per day in 2013!) continue to fine-tune the balance between personal and professional information that they Tweet. And not all leaders have transitioned to managing their own social media presence, but still find ways to employ the tool of Twitter to their advantage.

As Leslie Kwoh and Lisa Korn explained in *The Wall Street Journal,* "Many executives who tweet get a helping hand, either in the form of edits from their public-relations staff or ghostwritten posts. GE's Mr. Immelt, for instance, has a team that works to 'execute his vision' on Twitter, helping him draft tweets, according to company spokeswoman. The tweets are the result of a 'discussion' between Mr. Immelt and Deirdre

Latour, GE's senior director of communications, but 'it's his tone and vision,' she says.

"CEOs who do mind their own accounts have to steer clear of bashing competitors, disparaging customers or opining on polarizing topics like religion and politics. When she trains executives on social media, Amy Jo Martin, CEO and founder of social-media agency Digital Royalty Inc., says clients are 'fearful of sharing too much versus not sharing enough.' She advises executives to give followers a glimpse, not a guided tour, of their lives."[74]

Another way that new-school leaders build and expand upon their network is through *blogging*, whether on their own or company sites, or as an "influencer" invited to other platforms like the highly influential and professionalized LinkedIn or even *Huffington Post*.

As Lee Frederickson, PhD outlined as some of the concrete "bottom-line" benefits of blogging:

> ➢ *98% of business decision-makers read blogs, watch peer videos and listen to podcasts*

> ➢ *Firms getting 40-60% of their leads online grow 4 times faster than those generating no online leads.*

> ➢ *The greater the proportion of leads generated online, the greater the firm's profitability.*

> ➢ *The #1 technique among the fastest growing and most profitable firms is blogging.*

> ➢ *At some point in the buying process, 81% of all buyers go online to check out you or your firm.*

> ➢ *Either you have a compelling online persona that confirms your prized word-of-mouth referral or you don't.*

> ➢ *Make sure you develop a content strategy that makes a positive (and lasting) first impression online.*[75]

New-school leaders are taking their social media capacity from personal tools up to the level of their network and their brand's network, considering all of the applications and derivatives of basic messaging platforms that can enhance productivity. I discuss the ways in which new-school leaders use their digital and social media to their competitive advantage in Chapter 5. But at fundament, it is essential to be able to maximize your presence on social networks in order to deliver and improve on your leadership goals.

# H = High Energy

The dynamic business and technology environments in which we now live, work, and interact demand a great deal of leaders today. Standing out from the crowd amidst the constant inputs of information can seem daunting, all by itself. New-school leaders have many different sorts of guises and personalities, but *inside,* they are remarkably similar: they have high-energy drives to disregard challenges, overcome obstacles, and charge past defeat in their pursuit of that vision which motivates and compels them. In fact, problems seem to *fuel* them rather than sap their power or momentum.

The energy of new-school leaders is noted by everyone whom they encounter, from customers and stakeholders to staff and employees to informal community members and new contacts. Their energy is compelling to follow, and it is communicates the leader's willingness to pursue a vision vigorously, even in spite of pre-existing rules or outmoded systems. New-school leaders embrace a very high energy in order to deliver on their ambitions with a fearless and unique single-mindedness.[76]

Of course, with high energy comes high awareness: new-school leaders are always cognizant of the big picture, the total landscape, and they use their capacity to hold all that they see in balance. Stanford GSB Professor Robert Sutton has noted how research shows that high-energy leaders, those who accomplish a great deal, "have high positive <u>and</u> high negative affect, which means they're really optimistic and confident things will turn out in the end, *but* they're really, really worried about every little detail and how it's going to screw things up."[77]

High-energy leaders are also able to increase their efficiency through leveraging technology. This temperament matches the newest generation of colleagues and staff, since they too value action and more productive, efficient work plans so that they can have more personal time, and balance their professional and private lives. New-school leaders use some of that high energy to play! Think of Richard Branson ballooning around the world, or Google president Eric Schmidt enjoying life as a private plane pilot.

# I = Influence & Enrollment

**People buy into the leader before they buy into the vision.**
—John Maxwell

One of the core skills of a new-school leader is the ability to influence others to believe in and help manifest his or her unique vision for progress and success. This involves a combination of things including great listening and communication skills, as well as aspects of employee engagement, relationship management and even high energy! But negotiations with and persuasion of the many types and groups that a leader encounters in pursuit of influencing desired outcomes are both demanding and complex. Mastering a strategy of 21st-century influence is very different than it was under traditional leadership, where a direction could simply be dictated and everyone would hop to! [78]

It is not a new-school leader's *power position* that accomplishes what she wants done: it is her ability to *influence* people, both inside and outside of her association or institution, that determines her ultimate success. This begins by getting others to *enroll, trust, and respect* in her vision and integrity. Other tenets of leadership support her ability to influence, as well, including empathy for and appreciation of other points of view and cultures, along with deliberate communication which brings those views and communities to her project or purpose.

**Enrollment** occurs only after it is clear that a leader has recognized the potential impact of a decision or request on stakeholders or populations who may have very different values and priorities than her own. She will often employ her attention to diversity and inclusion, and the wisdom that she gleans from her D&I plan, in order to maximize enrollment in her vision.

This has become all the more important as new-school leaders' businesses and customers have become more global. A strategy, approach, or product that is appropriate or successful in the United States may need to be considered through another set of eyes, or changed altogether, in order to influence an African partner, or to get an Australian market to embrace or sign on to participate in it. Cultural sensitivities directly impact a new-school leader's success at influence and enrollment.[79]

Influence works in a positive as well as a negative way for new-school leaders, so they need to remain mindful of their impact in building corporate feeling. As British transformational leadership specialist Gordon Tredgold reminds us so simply, "People follow the leader's lead … If you look to blame people then you will create a blame culture. If you want a culture of respect, then look to respect the people in your team."[80]

Seems simple enough, but new-school leaders do need to remain mindful and intentional about the influence they wield and the values to which they ask their myriad stakeholders to subscribe. Loyalty and respect are *earned* by new-school leaders, and not automatically expected. Talent pools and stakeholders are influenced by the openness, transparency and clarity of communication offered by those leaders whom they seek to follow.

> *Lead and inspire people. Don't try to manage and manipulate people. Inventories can be managed but people must be lead.*
>
> —Ross Perot

New-school leaders are more successful in their efforts to enroll Millennials and Gen Y team members in particular when they have "green" initiatives, and when leaders attend clearly and specifically to an enterprise's impacts on the environment, as an institutional value. Equal treatment of women and men also generates positive influence: newer generations of employees have all grown up with professional working mothers, or they are ones, themselves, and so they expect both genders to have comparable value to their leadership, and demonstrably so.

New-school leaders are better able to enroll staff and employees to whom they offer the chance to grow and learn new things, whether it is direct leadership training, or technology and management skills development. This speaks to their interests and needs, but it also creates a culture of lifelong learning throughout a corporation. And leaders are better able to influence employees when they offer compensation other than money: it has been shown that today's staff is much more likely to enroll in the corporate vision of an enterprise that values their family time, their recreation, and their needs for flex travel or work location, in addition to providing fair pay.

Sometimes new-school influence looks much more hands-off than it once did. Leaders don't have all of the answers as to how best to do various jobs, and so the wise ones increase enrollment in their mission by giving their team members freedom and autonomous decision-making opportunities. Their staff and stakeholders are *more engaged with projects where they have ownership and responsibility*, so sometimes leaders accomplish much more by doing less![81]

*The Huffington Post*'s Director of Community, Tim McDonald, learned an interesting lesson recently about the intersection between new-school leadership and influence, as he engaged in a conversation with a cold and hungry homeless man named Joshua in New York City, and then posed a question while sharing his actions and observations with his social network, which led conversation and influence amongst his friends and followers.

"Sharing what you do can be more powerful than what you actually do," he concluded. "This didn't come from a message that was declared, or an order 'passed down,' it was shared with those around me. Leaders belong in the community, not above it.

"...Small ripples, repeated consistently, create waves ... I [asked] Jenn Shaw, founder of Bella Minds, how she would define leadership. Her response reminds me of what Joshua taught me, 'Leadership is helpfulness. You don't have to lead a million people, just someone.' It's the little ripples: Taking time to stop and talk to someone sitting on the street, sharing an experience with your friends or coworkers, or writing a post to help others realize they are leaders too. It just takes helping someone to become a leader.

"Joshua showed me ... leadership is not about raising yourself above others, it's being one with others. It's also not about affecting the masses; it's about affecting just one person. Leadership does not mean having followers; it's about having an impact, or influence, on those around you."[82]

# *P = Platinum Rule*

New-school leaders are much more attuned to the *Platinum Rule* than to the Golden Rule. The latter is certainly familiar, as it's also called the "ethic of reciprocity": to treat others as you would like them to treat you; concomitantly, this means <u>not</u> treating others in ways that you would <u>not</u> like to be treated (sometimes called the Silver Rule). Sliding up the list of precious metals, writers Tony Alessandra and Michael J. O'Connor have done the primary work of outlining the now popular Platinum Rule. It has grown in importance for new-school leaders because not everyone is *like* us, so <u>they</u> *don't want* to be treated the way <u>we</u> do!

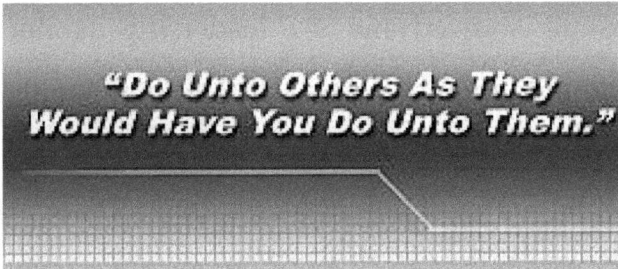

"Do Unto Others As They Would Have You Do Unto Them."

Put most simply: the Platinum Rule recommends that we treat others the way <u>*they*</u> *want* to be treated.[83] Like other qualities in the new-school leadership model, including those of empathy and inclusion, the Platinum Rule encourages leaders to remain keenly attuned to the styles and feelings of others as distinct from their own, and to respect those styles and feelings as having their own integrity and priority. As Alessandra explains it, "the focus of relationships shifts from 'this is what I want, so I'll give everyone the same thing' to 'let me first understand what they want and then I'll give it to them.'"[84]

The reason that I include this in my model is not just to update a common aphorism, but because the Platinum Rule looks at ways for new-school leaders to have productive relationships. It advocates treating people in ways that they appreciate, and encourages leaders to use language with employees and colleagues to which they relate. For example, some types of staff or stakeholders prefer a particularly touch-feely method of communication; while others respond better to the more direct and impersonal, or firm and forceful, style. The Platinum Rule asks that leaders recognize these as distinct differences without value judgment, and also that they themselves will be more successful by adopting different modes of communication, or methods of treatment, with different types of people, based on who they are and what they want.

Alessandra goes on to divide behavioral preferences into the four dominant styles of Director, Socializer, Relater and Thinker. Like other personality typing and evaluation systems, this is one that can be of great benefit to the new-school leader because it identifies the governing needs of each style, making it easier to address and adapt to members of each group; it also describes ways to approach them that are inspiring and productive.

So, for example, as Alessandra outlines in his book and website:

"**<u>Directors</u>** are driven by two governing needs: to control and achieve. Directors are goal-oriented go-getters who are most comfortable when they are in charge of people and situations. With Directors, in general, be efficient and competent. Because they are very time-sensitive, never waste their time. Be organized and get to the point. Give them bottom-line information and options.

"**Socializers** are friendly, enthusiastic "party-animals" who like to be where the action is. They thrive on the admiration, acknowledgment, and compliments that come with being in the lime-light. With Socializers, in general, be interested in them. Socializers thrive on personal recognition, so pour it on sincerely. Support their ideas, goals, opinions, and dreams. Try not to argue with their pie-in-the-sky visions; get excited about them. And remember: they are social-butterflies, so be ready to flutter around with them, and give them time to socialize. Avoid rushing into tasks.

"**Thinkers** are analytical, persistent, systematic people who enjoy problem-solving. Thinkers are detail-oriented, which makes them more concerned with content than style. Thinkers are task-oriented people who enjoy perfecting processes and working toward tangible results. Thinkers are time-disciplined, so be sensitive to their time. They need details, so give them data. With Thinkers, in general, be thorough, well-prepared, detail-oriented, business-like, and patient.

"**Relaters** are warm and nurturing individuals. They are the most people-oriented of the four styles. Relaters are excellent listeners, devoted friends, and loyal employees. Their relaxed disposition makes them approachable and warm. They develop strong networks of people who are willing to be mutually supportive and reliable. Relaters are excellent team players but risk-aversive so, with Relaters, in general, be non-threatening and sincere. Relaters are relationship-oriented, and want warm and fuzzy relationships, so take things slow, earn their trust, support their feelings, and show sincere interest. Talk in terms of feelings, not facts, which is the opposite of the strategy for Thinkers. Relaters don't want to ruffle feathers. They want to be assured that everyone will approve of them and their decisions. Give them time to solicit co-workers' opinions. Never back a Relater into a corner. It is far more effective to apply warmth to get this chicken out of its egg than to crack the shell with a hammer."[85]

The new-school leader who studies the ramifications of the Platinum Rule and applies them to his association or corporation is better able to organize work groups and to recognize ways to maximize the talents and capacities of his diverse types of stakeholders. Some personality types work better in combination with others; others are not so compatible in their approaches to projects, reports, or sorts of feedback so are better allied with team members who communicate and operate in a like-minded way.

Leaders that shine in these ten areas of "LEADERSHIP," and that cultivate the skills detailed throughout this chapter, are the most likely to be inspirational to their followers and successful in their companies. Many of these aspects can be embraced and practiced at any point: they don't need to be inborn in a 21ˢᵗ-century leader; we all have an opportunity to round out our leadership capacity by investigating and embracing various of these aspects.

In addition to this core formula, however, there are five "must-haves" that ensure success for any stellar and highly impactful new-school leader. In the next chapter, I go into those in some depth.

# *Leadership Spotlight*

## **Amazon Founder Jeff Bezos' Top 10 Leadership Lessons**

1. *"Base your strategy on things that won't change."*
2. *"Be willing to be misunderstood for long periods of time."*
3. *Obsess About Customers, Not Colleagues Or Competitors*
4. *"There are two kinds of companies: those that try to charge more and those that work to charge less. We will be the second."*
5. *"Determine what your customers need, and work backwards."*

# *Leadership Spotlight*

**<u>Jeff Bezos' Top 10 Leadership Lessons (*cont'd*)</u>**

6. *"Our culture is friendly and intense, but if push comes to shove we'll settle for intense."*

7. *"If you want to be inventive, you have to be willing to fail."*

8. *"In the old world, you devoted 30% of your time to building a great service and 70% of your time to shouting about it. In the new world, that inverts."*

9. *"Everyone has to be able to work in a call center."*

10. *"This is Day 1 for the Internet. We still have so much to learn."*[86]

# CHAPTER 3

# THE MUST-HAVES

*"If you want to build a ship, don't herd people together to collect wood and don't assign them tasks and work, but rather teach them to long for the endless immensity of the sea."*

—Antoine de Saint-Exupery

I like very much what "intentional leadership" expert and former Thomas Nelson Publishers CEO Michael Hyatt says about why we have leaders. He says, "Leaders exist to create a shift in reality.

"Without leaders, things drift along. They go where they want to go, following the path of least resistance. However, when this is not desirable—or acceptable—you hire, elect, appoint or become a leader. The leader's job is to overcome resistance and make things flow in a different direction. His or her job is to create a different reality."[87]

The change we want and the reality we need are led by new-school leaders. They have some core skills that set them apart, and that enable them to maintain a "trailblazing attitude." They set their sights on goals and find the ways to attain them through sharing a vision that will determine their organization's ideal direction, whether their company has a dozen members or millions.[88]

In this chapter, I look at the five foundational musthaves for any future leader.

## *Vision*

*Where there is no vision, the people perish.*

*—Proverbs 29:18*

The way that new-school leaders realize change is not just by *managing* it: they *cause* it. And they begin by articulating a vision for the future, something that they believe in and are compelled to push into reality. Vision is a leader's "new picture of the future," and the organizing principle around which goals are set and plans are made.[89]

Many organizations and managers outline a **vision statement** for their enterprise which describes, in words, "where and what an organization wants to be in the future."[90] This document is a standard component of institutional structure, but is not the same as a new-school leader's **vision.** Vision is about action, a compelling picture that is generated in the imagination of a new-school leader that inspires forward motion once it is shared with clarity and passion.

New-school leaders have very concise visions of the future; they need to be communicated broadly and effectively, of course, in order to be realized. Later in this chapter I go into the communication and management skills that accompany vision, as foundations of excellent leadership. But this is where it begins. As USC business professor and best-selling author Warren Bennis reminds us, "In order to take the organization to the highest possible level, leaders must engage their people with a compelling and tangible vision."[91]

A new-school leader develops her vision based first on an association's or corporation's mission. This vision includes the action steps or pathways through which her organization can attain the results that she imagines.[92]

**Vision** is absolutely essential to new-school leadership because, without it, a leader's staff and stakeholders are bound to lose focus and pursue inefficient actions or directions. Granted, there are other members of a leader's team who will and should work out the details of the how's and when's of manifesting each action plan, in order to attain the new-school leader's identified goals; leaders do collaborate with their teams on all of the essential next steps. But vision requires that a leader always maintain a macro-view of his company, marketplace, field, and global community in order to ensure success.[93]

Great new-school leaders love their work, and are deeply animated by and engaged in the daily process of realizing their mission and pursuing their vision. It is here that leaders really can make a contribution to the world and change it into a better place; they know and understand this fact. Vision isn't based on what has been: it is all about the very best that we can be. New-school leaders use vision to forge new paradigms, and to burst beyond what has been considered the norm in their company, industry, or sphere.[94]

## *Purpose: Why*

If **vision** is the idea of where a leader's association or organization is going, then **purpose** is **why** we follow that leader there. A new-school leader must concentrate on communicating their vision for each stakeholder in an enterprise, but, even better than the explanation, they also position everyone's work "as part of a larger big-story purpose." Xerox PARC guru John Seely Brown describes it this way: "The job of leadership today is not just to make money. It's to make meaning."[95]

"Why" we do anything is on the top tier of the hierarchy of human needs, as identified by Abraham

Maslow in his 1943 paper "A Theory of Human Motivation" in *Psychological Review.*[96] Self-actualization is a perceived need, the desire to know and realize someone's full potential. "What a man can be, he must be,"[97] as Maslow wrote, and this is why people follow new-school leaders.

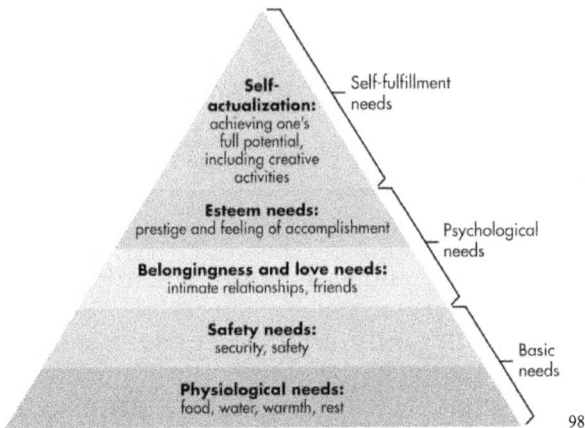

In part, our motivations for work and change are shifting in the 21st century. We are less enchanted with work for work's sake, or doing dull tasks long-term for purely financial reasons. Even though everyone wants and needs appropriate compensation and benefits, and even when we are able to negotiate a balance between work and personal life, still, more than ever, we want to know *why* we are undertaking our endeavors. So new-school leaders really examine the purpose for their own vision, the reason behind their mission, and the "why" for each project and strategic direction. Where the answers are connected to a higher good or a transformational contribution to community and planet, leaders find their message to followers all that more compelling.

As *Fast Company* co-founder Bill Taylor confirmed, the more executives, entrepreneurs, and talented individuals he got to know, the more he become convinced "that true happiness and genuine success ... came from losing yourself in a company you can believe in, a cause that you are prepared to fight for, and a commitment to a problem that has defied a solution."[99]

*Start with Why* author Simon Sinek writes extensively about the essential need for leaders to give their followers "something to believe in." When leaders need to inspire a team, in their quest to realize their visions, what is even more potent than a great work ethic and strong motivation is a *deep and clear sense of* **why.** "Great leaders inspire people to act. … Those who are able to inspire are those who give people a sense of purpose or belonging that has little to do with any external incentive or benefit to be gained … Those who are able to inspire will create a following of people— supporters, voters, customers, workers—who act … because they want to."[100]

A great contemporary example of nailing the "why" as a leader was when the iPod was developed by Steve Jobs and his team. Their "why" for this new device was that it "spoke to human love of music" through "a new type of human interaction with technology." The "why" was evident even in Jobs' slogan of "1,000 songs in your pocket," and made the iPod "something the entire world could appreciate as music moved toward the digital present."[101]

As a new-school leader sets about sharing his or her vision, their role is different from that of their managers, who will apply an organization's resources to do a job or attain established goals. What a new-school leader is doing is communicating a **common purpose**. "As author Seth Godin (*Poke the Box; The Icarus Deception*) says: Managers have employees. Leaders have followers."[102]

Having and sharing the "why" of a vision is sometimes considered a somewhat radical notion. Bill Deresiewicz, West Point lecturer and influential author of *A Jane Austen Education,* writes, "...for too long we have been training leaders who only know how to keep the routine going. Who can answer questions, but don't know how to ask them. Who can fulfill goals, but don't know how to set them. Who think about how to get things done, but not whether they're worth doing in the first place.

"What we don't have, in other words, are thinkers. People who can think for themselves. People who can formulate a new direction: for the country, for a corporation or a college, for the Army—a new way of doing things, a new way of looking at things. People, in other words, with vision."[103]

New-school leaders invite their team and stakeholders to join them in asking this question: "What is it that you want to create in the world around you that does not currently exist, that you are willing to endure personal sacrifice to bring to life?"[104] As they answer this together, they find the "why" to following a vision, and all of the energy they need to bring it to reality.

# *Passion*

*"Inspired leaders have congruency between their ambitions, intentions and inner core values."*
—John Demartini, "On Inspired Leaders."[105]

Passion shows that we care. It is something in our demeanor and expression that can clearly be seen: by our boards and our customers, by our teams and our stakeholders. It is a clear signal of our deep belief that we are doing important work which can bring about positive change, and it is an energy that inspires others to follow us in action and deed.[106]

Passion does not succeed in a vacuum. As Oracle CEO Mark Hurd reminds us, passion is but one component of new-school leadership. The "fiery and high-energy" expression of vision and personality must always be accompanied by hiring great people in the best positions to execute any "breakthrough strategy" that a leader designs and communicates about through their position.[107] Passion doesn't stand alone, but it is a powerful new-school leadership attribute, and an essential component for moving people and organizations towards change.

While part of being a new-school leader is believing passionately in the purpose or "why" of your vision,[108] equally important is your passion for those you work with and for. Starbucks CEO Howard Schultz uses the word "passion" in interviews frequently, and not about coffee! His passion is for "treating his employees with dignity and respect," because "happy employees lead to happy customers."[109] Sir Richard Branson, founder and CEO of the Virgin Group, also expresses in interviews his passionate commitment to everyone on his team, so that they can "elevate customer service."[110]

Maybe you don't see yourself as a leader like Sir Branson, who fires up rock-and-roll labels and pilots hot air balloons across stormy seas. There are many ways to express passion in an effective and inspiring manner. As Erika Anderson reminds us in her book *Leading so People Will Follow,* "passion isn't a wild, loud, take-no-prisoners quality. True passion requires honestly committing to something about which you feel deeply, and staying committed through difficult circumstances."[111] She describes her own five ways in which leaders indicate true passion:

*"Commit honestly*–Passionate leaders genuinely believe in what they espouse. People are touched and engaged by the genuineness of their passion.

*"Make a clear case without being dogmatic*–They convey the power of their belief without dismissing or belittling others' points of view.

*"Invite real dialogue about their passion*–Their passion is balanced with openness: they want to hear and integrate others' points of view.

**"*Act in support of their passion*–**They walk their talk: their day-to-day behaviors support their beliefs.

**"*Stay committed despite adversity and setbacks*–** Their commitment isn't flimsy; when difficulties arise, they hold to their principles and find a way forward."[112]

*Time Magazine* columnist Joel Stein wrote about his experience observing the leadership of a Hollywood fire chief named Captain Buzz Smith, and how truly passionate leaders include others in their commitment:

> *Everyone at his firehouse knows they are doing things exactly right. And that seems to make them both proud and assured. They would do anything for Captain Smith. Not because they love him— I'm not entirely sure that outside of the firehouse he could inspire them even to switch TV channels—but because his deep belief in his mission makes them also believe in that mission.*
>
> *What Captain Smith understands is that inspiring people through your personality is a risky, exhausting endeavor. But if you make people feel like you're going to help them accomplish something far bigger than you—not only saving lives, but living by a system that*

*provides dignity and pride—you can let your belief do the work for you.*[113]

A new-school leader *has* passion and *expresses* passion. They *live passionately* and they lead others to feel passion about their work, communities, and mission.

## Good Communication Skills

Compelling visions must be communicated, clearly and with passion, in order to create the change that a new-school leader desires. One of the communication challenges that we all face these days is all of the competing information, inputs, distractions, and data that swirl around our listeners, wherever they may be. As new-school leaders undertake to develop their top-notch communication skills, one of their major priorities is to share their vision in ways that are memorable, and that stand out from all the other ideas and inputs that bombard their teams constantly.[114]

Excellent communication skills dovetail with a leader's engagement and commitment to diversity and inclusion as well, of course, because communication is a dialogue by which they interact and share with team members and stakeholders across the full spectrum of their organization or enterprise. In a global marketplace with a multi-cultural workforce and client base, new-school leaders must constantly evolve new ways of communicating—that is, on a two-way basis—as well as connecting through emerging technologies and platforms. One key priority of excellent communication skills by any leader is to ensure consistency, but new-school leaders also must deliver their message in ways that are compelling to each level and background of their various stakeholders and team members, so that organizations and companies are motivated to take the right action in the very best way.[115]

There are many ways to communicate, and a significant component of this skills is great listening, something that I discuss in the next chapter. The most compelling means by which a new-school leader gets across his or her message is through directness and with transparency: great leaders embrace an openness about their agendas, along with candor and specificity; these are the strategies that will garner them the most success today.[116] Communication is always a dialogue, so encouraging feedback at the same time that any given message is delivered not only avails a leader of great ideas, but also uses communication skills to show respect for their stakeholders, which makes their message even more memorable.[117]

Communicating a message is done in many ways and, as I mentioned up in the section on social media presence, may be done on a wide variety of platforms. The key for a new-school leader is to make the commitment to share what is possible regularly and widely; that may mean communicating through writing and speech, or even singing and dance. The objective is to motivate people to be interested in what you are interested in, and in where you want to go.[118]

# *Leadership Spotlight*

## Exercise to develop and hone visionary communication skills

*—Debbie Zmorenski, Leader's Strategic Advantage consulting firm; 34-year executive with The Walt Disney World Company®.[119]*

"**Step 1:** Think of one challenge within your department, division or organization.

"**Step 2:** Imagine the big picture. Visualize the incredible future success that you will realize from the new and improved situation, as well as the benefits to the organization and to the employees. This is your chance to be a true visionary. No dream is too big or too fantastic. This is the "pie in the sky" result you are seeing.

"**Step 3:** Determine how you will communicate your vision. What words and phrases will you use? In what environment will you choose to communicate your vision—in a staff meeting, one on one, with supervisors and managers? How will you communicate the benefits to the staff and to the organization? Write down your ideas on paper.

# Leadership Spotlight

## Exercise to develop and hone visionary communication skills (*cont'd*)

"**Step 4:** Practice communicating what you have written. Make sure it sounds sincere. Practice out loud to yourself and to others. If you don't believe it, no one else will believe it either.

"If you use this exercise frequently, you will find that expressing your vision in a compelling and clear manner will soon feel very natural.

"When you are ready to communicate your vision to your employees, give them only the vision of success. Great leaders use vision as a tool to inspire and motivate, not to dictate. Do not give your employees the steps for achieving the vision, but let them determine the methods and tactics for achieving the goal. Great leaders know how to give the gift of vision and then step away."[120]

# *Management Skills*

> *No man will make a great leader who wants to do it all himself, or to get all the credit for doing it.*
> —Andrew Carnegie

New-school leadership requires solid skills for managing others, and for understanding the role and responsibilities of those managers who make up the executive ranks of their association, organization, or corporation. Leadership is not management but, that said, **leaders do nothing alone.** New-school leaders understand that essential management skills—the "order and consistency (of) drawing up formal plans, designing organization structures, and monitoring results against the plans,"[121]—are necessary to deliver on their ambitions.

Leaders establish the direction that their companies will take by starting with their concrete vision for a distinct and vibrant future. They then undertake an interactive development process with their management team members and stakeholders in order to plot their course of action. Through the techniques, skills, and strategies that I have outlined thus far, they build alignment and enrollment by communicating their vision, along with the "why"—the reasons for following them; they inspire their teams to persevere together through challenges. Leaders need to ensure that their projects are managed appropriately by people who think flexibly, creatively, and independently[122], even if managing directly is not something that they do themselves. "A leader is ultimately measured by his/her effectiveness, and because of that, the team surrounding them must be equipped and managed to support the goals of that leader."[123]

Many writers, from Burt Nanus to John Kotter to the late Abraham Zalznik, parse the differences between leadership and management, and try to delineate the variances. Ultimately, it must be agreed that both managers and leaders are essential forces within any organization or institution, even if there is "greater structure imbedded in management, and greater flexibility grounded in leadership."[124]

Leaders must have great ***management skills***, even if they don't have day-to-day management responsibilities, and they must recognize, support, and elevate the very best managers within their organizations in order to lead effectively.

As Stanford GSB Professor Hayagreeva Rao puts it, all of a leader's employees "need both story and structure. What I mean by story is lofty, inspirational messaging about excellence. But you also need the structure—the plumbing, if you will—the unglamorous parts … If you don't have both of those, you're never going to get anywhere."[125] Management skills provide "the plumbing."

Excellent management skills are the key to executing a leader's vision and strategy. New-school leaders need to "drive operational excellence," as Oracle CEO Mark Hurd summarizes it. And this attention to operations is what "brings the strategy alive with dynamic new products, sales teams that are highly intelligent and engaging, and brilliant new talent that sees the company as a terrific destination."[126]

He reminds leaders that, ideally, excellent management allows every person in your association or corporation "to work with the shared purpose of delighting customers, winning new business, creating fantastic new products, and identifying and exploiting opportunities well ahead of competitors."[127]

New-school managing involves motivating people, optimizing processes, and mobilizing resources, which include both human and non-human assets, throughout an entire organization. It involves identifying the strengths of each team member, distributing duties, and developing strategies to work through weaknesses. But while managers engage on all levels of a project, mission, or program, new-school leaders need to strive to maintain that "macro view of any given situation."[128]

Stanford GSB Professor Rao described excellent management as "connect and cascade ... You connect people so that you cascade the right behaviors throughout the organization ... When the connections inside organizations are weak or atrophied, if people aren't connecting, your ignorance multiplies."[129]

Graduate School of Business research into new-school management skills for leaders that help to maximize organizational capacity while minimizing conflict amongst potentially competitive or ambitious managers drew three conclusions on ways to forge a "path toward shared power and clear roles" for management:

1. **"Define, discuss and reinforce roles."** New-school management involves helping to ensure that each team member knows their role and standing, including succession, and that those roles fully embrace and acknowledge each manager's expertise. As they write, "a person who feels confident in his or her role is less likely to feel threatened," so new-school leaders support recognition and deference to specific skills and responsibilities amongst their managers.

2. **"Establish shared decision-making."** Good management involves encouraging teams to share power by collaborating on decisions. "Democratic decision-making styles, such as agreeing by consensus or informal votes" work,

as does the "concept of servant leadership" or the participatory model which we have been discussing here, in this book.

3. **"Provide conflict training and create a culture of respect.** Management teams that have sufficient training in conflict management skills are better at recognizing conflict and addressing the real underlying issues. Power struggles often arise in discussion of tasks or seemingly mundane process matters, such as what day of the week meetings will be held. Teams can establish a culture of respect in those discussions; or find creative ways to expand the hierarchy pie, so that each person in the team has power, though perhaps not in the domain he or she wants. Recognizing which team members are engaged in a power struggle and resolving it quickly and respectfully is artistry possessed by a few great leaders."[130]

Finally, as I did mention earlier, a key element of the new-school leader's management skills is to "delegate the important tasks" sometimes.[131] This also builds respect and appreciation on all levels of your team, and encourages autonomous thinking and creativity for the organization or enterprise.

◆

*We can't own and control this. We have to turn loose of the steering wheel and let others be part of shaping it.*[132]

—Bob Writer, Founder
Dallas Social Venture Partners

Every great new-school leader possesses, emphasizes, and develops their "must-have" attributes. These help to support their practice of participatory, inclusive and non-authoritarian 21st century leadership. Mastering this approach does not *just* result in happier stakeholders and more satisfied leaders. Deployed effectively, new-school leadership also helps you to gain a **commanding competitive advantage.**

The new-school leadership model is so successful at supporting leaders to maximize their opportunities for success that I like to call it "the unfair advantage." Let's look at the ways to activate your leadership capacity to the ultimate advantage for your association or business in the next chapter.

# Leadership Spotlight

**Oprah Winfrey Leadership Wisdom.**[133]

1. *"The thing you fear most has no power. Your fear of it is what has the power. Facing the truth really will set you free."*

2. *"I feel that luck is preparation meeting opportunity."*

3. *"Nobody's journey is seamless or smooth. We all stumble. We all have setbacks. It's just life's way of saying, 'Time to change course.'*

4. *"Turn your wounds into wisdom."*

5. *"The big secret in life is that there is no big secret. Whatever your goal, you can get there if you're willing to work."*

# *Leadership Spotlight*

### *Oprah Winfrey Leadership Wisdom (cont'd)*

6. *Feel the power that comes from focusing on what excites you."*

7. *"The key to realizing a dream is to focus not on success but significance–and then even the small steps and little victories along your path will take on greater meaning."*

8. *"I believe the choice to be excellent begins with aligning your thoughts and words with the intention to require more from yourself."*

9. *"The greatest discovery of all time is that a person can change his future by merely changing his attitude."*

10. *"You CAN have it all. You just can't have it all at once."*

# CHAPTER 4

# GAINING THE UNFAIR ADVANTAGE

When leaders, or companies, have skills or assets that no one else has, and which help them to be so strong or so dominant that competitors can't touch them, this is oftentimes described as the "unfair advantage." In our highly competitive marketplace, where the landscape is crowded with myriad demands on our customers' attention and our funders' resources, each association and company seeks to identify and cultivate their own unique "unfair advantage." New-school leaders know that everyone needs at least one, these days, and maybe more than one, in order to dominate their niche and lead their organizations to success.

As John Neishem, author of *The Power of Unfair Advantage* explains, "Unfair advantage is the Holy Grail," and "enables ideas to become world-class enterprises, and corporations to become icons."[134] It is what powers organizations to become the leader in their market and we all know that, bottom line, which is the singular goal and supreme purpose of every stakeholder in an enterprise or endeavor.

A company's or leader's unfair advantage can take many forms and come from a variety of sources but, ultimately, it's looked at as that "secret sauce" that may defy a specific, generalizable definition, but for which there is definitely a new-school recipe.[135] Leaders use this "sauce" to their advantage as much as possible, as they shape their visions and set strategy for their businesses. This chapter looks at some of the key ingredients that new-school leaders have at their disposal.

I do make a distinction between your unfair advantage and a Unique Selling Proposition, or USP, which is your answer to the question, "why should I buy from/work with you?" in the wake of myriad options or choices.[136] As *SmartPassiveIncome* guru Pat Flynn reminds us, "You definitely need a USP, but a USP is not your unfair advantage. It's how your business will stand out of the crowd, but a USP is not the skills or assets that can help you get there. You can't sell your skills, but you can and should absolutely use them to build and shape your business."[137]

Let's look at how to use new-school leadership strengths in order to gain the unfair advantage in your marketplace.

# Digital & Social Media

When new-school leaders maximize their understanding and application of digital and social media to their vision and strategy, they leapfrog over competitors in today's landscape. Beyond just having a social media presence, leaders can discover essential trends and enhance their communication with customers and team members in ways critical to their success. In addition, the new tools available to leaders in the digital and social media space offer opportunities to far outpace others in their specific niche or market.

Through social media, for example, new-school leaders can observe the constant customization of their customers' tastes and products, from the ways that they design their playlists and sports shoes to their Pinterest bulletin boards for what they, uniquely, love. As Patti Johnson explains in her new book *Make Waves: Be the One to Start Change at Work and Life,* "this growing trend drives the shift from 'one size fits all,' or your market segment, to 'one size fits me.'"[138] So, new-school leaders are leveraging social media to deliver personalized messages and product, as well as to glean critical data about the personalities and desires of customers, clients, and competitors, including very fine-tuned and rapidly developing details.

Another tool amongst the new-school leader's cache of new media tools is the social graph, a digital tool that Bonobos CEO Andy Brown claims is the single thing that makes his brand possible, but also that is making "the world a more personal place."[139] It is a tool that new-school leaders can employ in order to build their digital brands and to create in-person store experiences.

The *social graph* is a graphic depiction of personal relations between internet users. It's been referred to by CBS News (describing the original Facebook social graph) as "the global mapping of everybody and how they're related."[140]

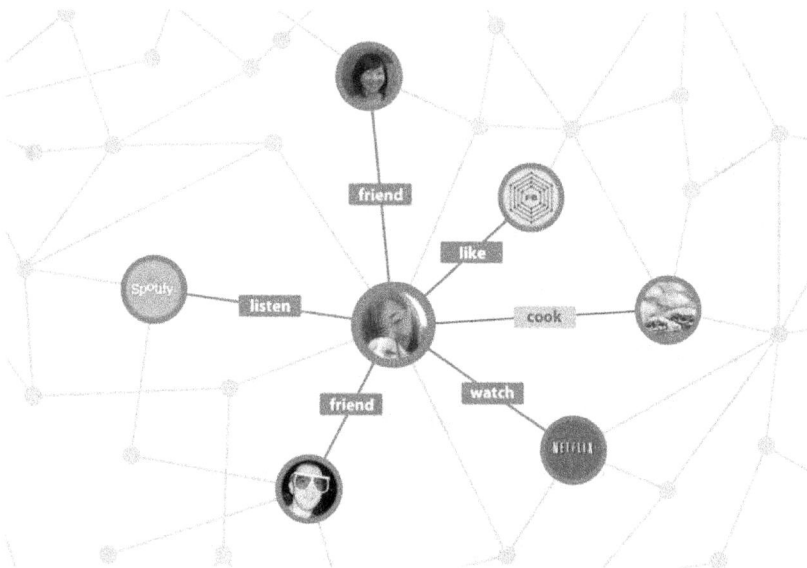

*Social Graph[141]*

The next-level iteration may be Twitter co-founder Biz Stone's brand new social media app Jelly, which was introduced in January 2014, and which employs photos and friends to find answers to questions that can't be easily unearthed through traditional search engines. Instead of computer algorithms like Google's, Jelly relies on human knowledge to help users find the answers that they seek, and each question must be accompanied with an image that users can even draw on with their fingers, where helpful.[142] According to Stone, the app works in ways similar to LinkedIn, where "second degree" connections to your own social media contacts appear in the answer feed to any question. "Everyone's mobile," Stone says. "Everyone's connected. So if you have a question, there's somebody out there that knows the answer."[143]

As he told *Vanity Fair* in April 2014, "In Jelly's test period ... a father desperate to diagnose his two-year-old child's mysterious phobia soon received a cure from a stranger online. A woman driven insane by a TV with a fatal flaw that every technician had failed to fix sent a picture of the back of the set to Jelly—and the problem was magically solved in a few seconds by another thoughtful stranger."[144]

"Whenever you build something," he told CNN at the popular music and new media conference South by Southwest (SxSW), "the creativity in humanity comes out. I love it when I'm seeing answers to questions where people are only drawing on the photo. They're not even using language. Somebody asked, 'How do you do a screenshot on a Mac?' and all the person (answering) did was circle the three keys you touch. It was wonderful."[145] He hopes that this "social search engine" will continue to connect people in ways that new-school leaders can leverage to maximize advantage.[146]

New-school leaders can also activate social media as their 21st-century "grapevine," which is critically important for brands and products right now. *Word of mouth* has become the salient communication method amongst our communities and customers, so new-school leaders know the impact of this social media trend. According to an Ernst & Young study called *This Time*

*It's Personal,* "Research tells us that we listen to the recommendations of those we know much more than to campaigns or packaged communications ... Peer recommendations—not paid-for advertising, whether on social media platforms or in print—are what count."[147] New-school leaders use their social media presence to develop a word-of-mouth strategy for their vision and their products, and also to *"crowd source"* or reach out to customers or broad, diverse employee networks for ideas and new designs.

New-school leaders are also finding ways to harness the "peer power" available in social media as a way to find strategies that can develop areas of change or solve core challenges without traditional hierarchies. Where aspects of their business can be crowd-sourced and designed by a broader group, new-school leaders are also using this social media tool to build engagement.

Social media tools can also streamline business practices in ways that enhance a leader's competitive advantage. The rapid advances in communication technology are permitting companies to encourage virtual sharing and collaboration from places all around the world. They can seem like wide-ranging challenges to leaders, at times, but new-school leaders find ways to leverage *virtual collaborations* and *crowdworking platforms* into exciting ways to advance their vision and business initiatives.[148]

In enterprises large and small, the *corporate website* has become a key branding, marketing, and interactive communication platform of critical importance to all aspects of the business. New-school leaders are cognizant of the internet as their 21$^{st}$-century market, and their website as a business edifice and brand image. Diversity and inclusion are easy to identify and promote in this space, as well as to undermine, through the optics and messages in digital and social media, so leaders need to be mindful of the full picture that they paint with their words and images.

Social media is also having a strong impact on the ways in which we do business in the areas of hiring and recruitment. A new-school leader's management of their company's *mobile media* presence is another critical aspect of their preparedness and opportunity. As the professional talent juggernaut site LinkedIn asks in its introduction to it *Online Recruiting Playbook,* "Your candidates are on mobile. Are you?"

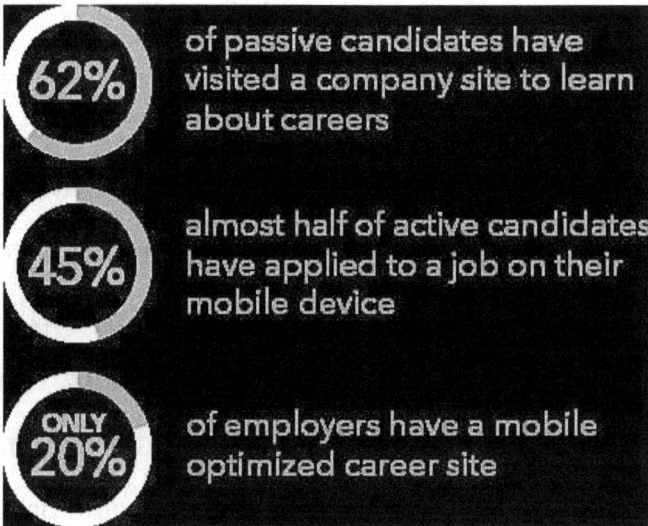

| | |
|---|---|
| **62%** | of passive candidates have visited a company site to learn about careers |
| **45%** | almost half of active candidates have applied to a job on their mobile device |
| **ONLY 20%** | of employers have a mobile optimized career site |

149

A leader and his company need to invest in and optimize their mobile media strategy as part of their social media presence, too, because talent are now joining companies through mobile recruiting experiences, accessing career websites via mobile, and communicating with a business's HR department on mobile.

A new-school leader's next top staff hires, team members and potential candidates want to **learn** about his or her company culture and job opportunities through mobile technology, so it needs to be mobile-friendly (e.g. no Flash; and it should look good on any screen). They want to **apply** for opportunities from their mobile devices, and since they don't store their resumés on their phones OR want to fill out a zillion questions on a small touch screen, leaders now need to link professional social profiles into their application process in a seamless way, in order to accommodate social-media HR.

Finally, candidates now also want to **engage** with companies through mobile, once they are in the HR system. Designing easy-to-read emails that have clear calls to action make mobile communication savvy and practical. New-school teams even use mobile for interviews now, whether via Skype or WhatsApp applications, or by using social media tools to send interviewees directions and traffic alerts in advance of face-to-face visits.[150]

Social media is a sophisticated set of tools, but when deployed carefully and well, they can definitely enhance a new-school leader's capacity in ways that deliver an "unfair advantage" to their business. The key is to activate digital and social media to connect with your community, which is the network of customers and partners who make up the ecosystem of your users. Each platform helps you to add value to your product by employing it to gain unique access to your customers and expert endorsements, and then to build and proclaim your leading reputation for customer service.[151]

As Twitter co-founder Biz Stone writes in his book *Things a Little Bird Told Me*, the "triumph" of social media and its revolutionary powers is not a "triumph of technology but of humanity": they can help you "change our lives" and "change our world."[152]

## *Understanding Trends*

*One of the tests of leadership is the ability to recognize a problem before it becomes an emergency.*

—Arnold Glasow

Since a key tenet of new-school leadership is staying a head of the curve, the opportunity arises to gain an unfair advantage by staying very attuned to trends in your field and the broader socio-economy, and then understanding how they apply to your business or association.

True, new-school leaders do lead change in order to set trends in their unique fields or spheres, but at the same time, they swim in a culture of broader trends— directions and opportunities that impact those core strategies that must be set for their organizations. Understanding trends begins with flexibility and keen observation. Essential is the ability to consider multiple perspectives, in order to make sense of what's going on, and the willingness to receive information from conflicting sources. Understanding trends requires the distillation of tremendous complexity, these days.[153]

Change will continue to occur at an accelerated pace throughout our world; how this is impacting our customers' needs and our communities' tastes will have critical impact on a new-school leader's strategies for product development as well as for customer and employee engagement, and will determine whether those strategies are sustainable and can keep pace with guaranteed constant upheavals.[154] A failure to understand the impact of trends, as Oracle President Marc Hurd explains, will inevitably lead leaders to feel like they are constantly "playing catch-up with competitors, always struggling to find new sources of revenue, and all too frequently seeing market share taken by competitors that are far more in tune with customers, opportunities, and structural trends."[155]

The key indicator that a new-school leader comprehends and embraces the trends relevant to each aspect of her business is whether or not she has formulated a strategy for her enterprise that responds to change, that adjusts when and as soon as necessary, and that empowers managers and team members throughout the company to perceive and address whenever something is headed in a new and relevant direction. [156]

One trend that social media has driven so forcefully, for example, is the way in which we now work together. Since we have witnessed "the dramatic effect of leveling the playing field by allowing anyone to have a voice, platform, or following," new-school leaders need to forge strategy that addresses the consequence of this trend that is swiftly turning hierarchies upside down.

Patti Johnson writes in her new book *Make Waves,* "Our stories and information don't need to be filtered through an "expert" or an official source. The hierarchy and the command-and-control environment in business are giving way to a culture with more flexible and collaborative leadership unrelated to title or years of experience. An organic, flexible change plan is essential."[157]

The lifelong learning tenet of new-school leadership applies directly to noticing, evaluating, and then understanding trends. So will excellent communication skills, because, where the lines of dialogue are truly open, leaders are able to hear and understand suggestions and information from every level of stakeholder, and from every customer, employee, or manager who may have a great idea.

Finally, as Bonobos CEO Andy Dunn deduced, unfair advantage in such a competitive and quickly evolving environment requires not just attunement to trends and great ideas, but also an analysis as to whether a specific new-school leader is the right match to address *that* trend or idea. For example, he says, "before Bonobos, I worked on an idea for a personalized content magazine, similar to Instapaper. There was no reason I was the right person to build that business, and therefore I didn't. People say great companies are built by great teams. I think that's true. But I look for more than just great teams and great ideas; I like ideas that are uniquely authentic for that particular team.[158] A leader's passion is best applied to that opportunity and trend that she is ideally suited to embrace.

Once you understand the trends, you'll understand what's perfect for you to pursue with your high energy and full commitment.

# *Ability to Handle Change*

*Anyone can hold the helm when the sea is calm.*
—Publilius Syrus

Harvard's John Kottler has said, "Leadership is very much related to change. As the pace of change accelerates, there is naturally a greater need for effective leadership." Much of this book has addressed the fact that, in order to be a new-school leader in such volatile and uncertain times, change is handled through a mastery of influence, both within a business, and to a wide network outside of a company[159] The concomitant fact in the new-school paradigm is that *leadership has changed,* too. The ultimate "unfair advantage," then, accrues to those leaders who have changed enough to **expect change,** rather than think that they are ever out in front of it.

The driver of this aspect of leadership is the breadth *and* rate of change. Globalization, the new and ever-expanding mesh of links between people and products, events and activities, compounded by the constant evolution of technology and innovation each impact an element of change that should be considered by every leader. Expect to be surprised every day by a new invention, maybe one that shakes up your industry from top to bottom! Expect that your workplace *will* become more culturally, racially, and ethnically diverse with each hire. Expect that unlikely collaborations, new relations, and unusual partnerships may offer opportunities that never made sense, before. Expect new markets to become available for your exploitation that didn't even exist when your enterprise began. And expect the untoward impact of your clients, your team members and the media, as their power to support or deter your every initiative will continue to grow at warp speed.[160]

The Dale Carnegie Leadership Institute advocates for drafting a leadership plan specifically for *change*. In order to handle change in the most advantageous way, so that it becomes an institutional asset and "unfair advantage," it helps to devise a change leadership plan that:

> ➤ *Avoids the most common change leadership mistakes;*
> ➤ *Recognizes the elements of and applies a model for change engagement;*
> ➤ *Defines the type of changes currently occurring in the organization; and.*
> ➤ *Identifies ways to lead others and manage ourselves during organizational change.* [161]

# Great Listening Skills

As Twitter co-founder Biz Stone writes in the introduction to his new book *Things a Little Bird Told Me,* "the greatest skills that I possessed and developed over the years was the ability to listen to people: the nerds at Google, the disgruntled users of Twitter, my respected colleagues, and, always, my lovely wife."[162]

New-school leaders have developed empathy, and honed solid two-way communication skills. The "two" in two-way is really about *listening.* It involves listening to voices loud and soft, lofty and low, "important" and emerging, and hearing what is said across the full spectrum of stakeholders in a leader's enterprise. Now more than ever, as I've shown, great information or ideas or adjustments can come from anywhere on the new-school leader's landscape.

Great listening is one of the best ways to understand trends, in fact, and to learn what is really going on, both inside and outside of one's company. It involves remaining "receptive to new ideas, criticisms and different perspectives."[163]

Listening also involves parsing messages in order to develop an accurate understanding of reality and truth. Many leaders think that they are "the repository of all truth," especially successful ones! And even when they aren't that out of touch or ego-centric, it is still possible to keep hearing "truth" only from their faithful followers, which tends towards being self-perpetuating, diluted or one-sided[164] Or, worse, may be highly sanitized versions of information. As Ivey Business School Dean Carol Stephenson reminds us, "no-one, including your employees or partners, likes to admit that they made a mistake. It is natural to sugar-coat the bad news. But if you do not have all the facts and the truth, how can you solve the problem?"[165] Great listening involves really hearing **the truth**.

Professors Robert Sutton and Hayagreeva Rao tell a great listening story, based on their research at Stanford GSB.

"We talked to a top executive who turned around the largest company in Australia, who had the top 100 or so folks write him a 2-page memo about what they should do to turn around the organization. And he said, 'I just talked to each person for an hour, and took the best ideas.'"[166]

It seems simple enough, and yet, had the new-school Australian leader not really listened to the input offered, he would have lost the opportunity to discern the very best direction and means by which to save his company.

In the same way that power can affect a new-school leader's capacity for empathy, so too does it stand in the way of great listening. In order to put these skills to maximum "unfair advantage," in order to hear the essential voices on all levels and at the most critical junctures in order to understand and respond to trends, leaders need to mitigate the "panoptic effect of power on people." Despite the fact that their power as leaders by definition changes them, nevertheless they need to try to hear the goals and desires of others, and really absorb their various perspectives, plus listen to other people's feelings, as well.[167] Leaders who don't will swiftly undermine their competitive advantages.

## *Like-able*

When people like and respect their leaders, they want to work for them. New-school leaders combine their empathy, inclusion, and relationship management into the presentation of an approachable personality that is supremely **likeable,** in order to gain an "unfair advantage" over less open, accessible leaders.

The power behind likeability is that it builds trusting relationships with stakeholders and team members, and we have already discussed the ways in which "trust is the bedrock of leadership."[168] In a recent *Psychology Today* article that lists the top six reasons why bosses fail, unlikeable qualities like being "a bully," "inauthentic," being "punitive … and flying off the handle," along with other poor or boorish behavior account for most every reason that employees hate them.[169]

Remember, *a real unfair advantage is one that cannot easily be copied or bought.* The ideal advantages for new-school leaders are those that are very hard to replicate, and your unique, welcoming and open personality can be one of your very best assets, in this regard. Likeability is not just about "people-pleasing," or avoiding the rough decisions. As author Dave Kerpen explains in his book *Likeable Leadership,* the key is your "commitment to treat others with respect."[170] He, too, asserts that we follow the Platinum Rule in order to enhance likeability, and to create environments of respect and positivity that are invariably more successful than any others.

This may seem like an unusual consideration for the new-school leader, but think about all of the attention we give to likeability in other aspects—all aspects, really—of our business: our products, our practices, our services, our image. Another consequence of social media is that customer feedback is rapid, is shared broadly with the general public, and can have a marked impact on our enterprise's success or failure. We want to generate positive response to who we are and what we do—so, being likeable, as a company, is a distinct "unfair advantage!"

I apply this same argument to new-school leaders. Openness, transparency, and likeability actually help leaders to make tough decisions, too; uncomfortable facts or determinations are better received and understood by employees and team members when they come from a leader whom they trust. The new-school leader's social media presence can help to build that platform of likeability by letting people in on the reasons to respect and follow you.

Most leaders already understand their likeability, or they did at one time, because they were selected, supported, and mentored along the way to their position of power. In addition to the other tenets of this new-school leadership model that grow leaders towards success and great results, being likeable is no doubt something that has already been recognized within you, along the way.[171] Your "unfair advantage" comes from remembering and cultivating that aspect of your leadership personality, even once you have risen to the top, as it can continue to serve you in important and impactful ways.

As Duke's Fuqua School of Business professor Dorie Clark summarizes about Kerpen's approach, "ultimately … likeability comes from within. In order to be likeable and successful, he says, 'we need to be the kind of person we would like.' That means embracing authenticity, transparency, responsiveness, and other principles you value. 'If I'm completely honest with everyone I talk to, I never have to worry about whether I'd like myself, because we all appreciate honesty.'

"'The key thing is having perspective on what is most important to you," says Kerpen, who writes often about his devotion to his family. 'I have every single one of my managers do an activity with their teams where they write their obituaries. You're going to have to think about what you want to be remembered for in this world. I'd challenge everyone out there to think about what they really want that obituary to look like, and make sure you live your life in a way that will generate that.'"[172]

Becoming a more likeable leader will redound to you and your unique "unfair advantage."

## *Leadership Spotlight*

**New GM CEO Mary Barra told her** *Stanford Alumni magazine* **that her** *"job is to keep up with the technology advancement so that consumers are able to choose. So if we as a company have the right technology that allows us to deliver fuel economy, yet still offer a range of size and products to meet people's needs and wants, that's how we win."[173]*

Barra is the first female CEO of General Motors, or any major automobile manufacturer, and part of the scant 4% of female chief executives of Fortune 500 companies. Her style is distinctly inclusive, and always involves uniquely effective work teams in ways that have increased engagement and connected her employees back to GM so that they generate innovative ideas and penetrate the exploding diverse markets. She sends a signal that being an inclusive leader *"is no longer an option to consider; it's a must-do for the future success of any company."[174]*

# CHAPTER 5

# SUMMARY & CONCLUSIONS

*A leader is best when people barely know he exists, when his work is done, his aim fulfilled, they will say: we did it ourselves.*

—Lao Tzu

One of the things that I most enjoy about my path as a leader is the very first part of my new-school model: being a lifelong learner. Likely you are one, as well, as you consider the ideas for leadership development and success that are covered in this book.

I think that each one of us who leads and who aspires to lead better finds themselves enjoying or excelling in some of the aspects outlined in my model perhaps more than others. That is what is exciting to me about the opportunity to continuously learn and grow. We can identify and expand on those skills and capacities that are working, the ones that are more natural for us or better developed, but we can also begin to explore and exercise some aspects of the new-school leadership model that may be less familiar or new.

Remember those paltry statistics about how few Fortune 500 CEOs are using social media!? You know that those numbers will change rapidly, as will many leadership strategies within those companies. Do you know what else will change? The *make-up* of the Fortune 500: each year it will welcome companies that are led by new-school leaders, because existing enterprises that fail to embrace diversity and inclusion, engagement, influence and enrollment, or social media opportunities will invariably fade in influence.

As a leader who is committed to personal development, you have every opportunity to excel in your endeavors at whatever association, department, or organization you head. Considering, embracing, and manifesting the "must-haves" and leadership model elements presented here can only help you to amplify your ambitions to make change.

I was inspired, myself, by a recent blog in the *Harvard Business Review* which reminded me that, despite all the solitary, personal learning and reflection and visioning that we do as leaders, and all of the "great man/great woman" stories that we tell about individual change leaders like Dr. Martin Luther King or even Steve Jobs, in fact, all true, inspirational leadership and extraordinary accomplishments start **in community, working with** and **for** others.[175] We may undertake our professional development alone but what we seek to accomplish or move or sell or change is rarely done without a wide network of stakeholders and mentors. The victories to which we aspire are destined to have broad impact and service many. The community that I can improve and work with inspires me, daily.

I hope that *New-School Leadership* supports your every effort at leading exceptional and profitable change.

# ABOUT THE AUTHOR

D.A. (David Anthony) Abrams is an author, speaker, and advisor who currently serves as the Chief Diversity & Inclusion Officer for the United States Tennis Association (USTA), formerly in White Plains, New York and now in Orlando, Florida.

Abrams has been involved in tennis since being introduced to the sport via the National Junior Tennis & Learning, formerly National Junior Tennis League (NJTL) of Philadelphia. As a junior player, he excelled, earning national rankings in the United States Tennis Association, and the American Tennis Association. Good grades along with his hard work on the tennis court earned him a tennis scholarship to attend Millersville University of Pennsylvania. After graduation, he put his accounting degree to good use at Control Data Corporation based in Minneapolis, MN.

Missing tennis, Abrams returned to Philadelphia after four years in the Twin Cities to serve as the Recruitment Director and Head Tennis Professional at the Arthur Ashe Youth Tennis Center (AATYC). While at AAYTC, he launched Dave Abrams Tennis Services, a full-service tennis company that offered tennis instruction to adults and juniors, as well as International Tennis Tours. Abrams has been a certified member of the United States Professional Tennis Association, and Professional Tennis Registry since the early 1990s.

In 1993, Abrams moved to White Plains, NY to join the United States Tennis Association (USTA), where he is now Chief Diversity & Inclusion Officer. He has also served in the following capacities: Executive Director of two USTA Sections (Eastern, 2006-2012) and Missouri Valley (1997-2000); Director of Community Outreach (2000-2006); and National Coordinator, NJTL & Minority Participation (1993-1996).

As a board member of the Alzheimer's Association-Hudson/Rockland/Westchester, NY Chapter (July 2009 to June 2013), Abrams served in the following roles: Chair, Audit Committee; Member, Compensation Committee; Member, Nominating Committee; and Member, Development Committee. In addition, he played an active role in the New York Society of Association Executives (NYSAE; 2010-2011) as a member of the Membership and Education Committees. It should be noted that Abrams is a Certified Association Executive (CAE).

Abrams believes in life-long learning, and loves to read. He also loves to write, and is the author of

*Diversity & Inclusion: The Big Six Formula for Success*, as well as *Certified Association Executive Exam: Strategies for Study & Success*. Both books are available wherever best-selling titles are sold.

Abrams enjoys travelling with his wife (Shelia D. Abrams), and has visited all of the states within the United States with the exception of four. Countries that he has visited outside of the U.S. include: Australia, Morocco, Denmark, Sweden, Norway, England, China, France, Italy, Thailand, Brazil, Costa Rica, Jamaica, Mexico, Canada, Spain, Indonesia, and the Bahamas.

Over the years, Abrams has made many media appearances, including: "America's Black Forum," hosted by James Brown, to discuss the mission of the USTA's Community Outreach department; a Satellite Media Tour (i.e. 15 Markets across the United States) with tennis legend Zina Garrison, to discuss African-Americans in tennis and the National Junior Tennis League; and CNBC's "Rivera Live," as a panelist, to discuss the impact of Venus and Serena Williams on tennis participation among multicultural groups.

Recent print articles include:

❖ "Exec of the Future: D.A. Abrams—Different Strokes" (http://associationsnow.com/2012/09/exec-of-the-future-different-strokes/), and

❖ "Serving Up Diversity: The USTA's D.A. Abrams–Diversity Executive" (http://diversity-executive.com/articles/view/serving-up-diversity-the-u-s-tennis-association-s-d-a-abrams).

Please feel free to connect with Abrams:

Twitter - @DAAbrams1

(https://twitter.com/DAAbrams1)

Instagram—DAAbrams1

(www.instagram.com/DAAbrams1)

LinkedIn - D.A. Abrams, CAE

(*www.linkedin.com/pub/d-a-**abrams**-cae/7/a04/459*)

Facebook - David Anthony Abrams

(https://www.facebook.com/david.a.abrams)

◆◆◆◆◆◆

# REFERENCES & ENDNOTES

[1] AchieveGlobal with Craig Perrin, Sharon Daniels et al. *Developing the 21ˢᵗ Century Leader.* Tampa, Florida: AchieveGlobal World Headquarters, 2010.

[2] DiMattia, Ernie. "Leadership vs. Management," quoting Warren Bennis, *On Becoming a Leader.* New York: Basic Books, 2009.

[3] Demartini, John. "On Inspired Leaders." *Business Brief Magazine/* bbrief.co.za.

[4] MacDonald, Matthew. "Leadership–Influencing Through Relationship." *BusinessBlogsHub.com.* May 2011.

[5] Ekaterina Walker. "The Power of Purpose." *The Huffington Post.* 8 Dec 2013.

[6] "Can One Person Make a Difference?" *www.businessblogshub.com.* February 2014.

[7] William Pollard. BrainyQuote.com, Xplore Inc, 2014. http://www.brainyquote.com/quotes/quotes/w/williampol163253.html, accessed March 16, 2014.

[8] "The Evolution of Leadership." *MindResources Institute of Learning and Innovation.* Vol 2, Issue 2, pp 1-9.

[9] Green, Holly. "Leadership: Then and Now." *www.Forbes.com.* 30 Aug 2011.

[10] Stephenson, Carol, O.C. "How Leadership Has Changed." *Ivey Business Journal/From The Dean.* July-August 2011.

[11] Denning, Steve. "The Key Missing Ingredient In Leadership Today." *www.Forbes.com.* 27 July 2012.

[12] Denning, Steve. "The Key Missing Ingredient In Leadership Today." *www.Forbes.com.* 27 July 2012.

[13] Denning, Steve. "The Key Missing Ingredient In Leadership Today." *www.Forbes.com.* 27 July 2012.

[14] Denning, Steve. "The Key Missing Ingredient In Leadership Today." *www.Forbes.com.* 27 July 2012.

[15] Cole, Neil. "Old v. New Leadership: A Study in Contrasts."

[16] Green, Holly. "Leadership: Then and Now." *www.Forbes.com.* 30 Aug 2011.

[17] Stephenson, Carol, O.C. "How Leadership Has Changed." *Ivey Business Journal/From The Dean.* July-August 2011

[18] The Evolution of Leadership." *MindResources Institute of Learning and Innovation.* Vol 2, Issue 2, pp 1-9.

[19] "The Evolution of Leadership." *MindResources Institute of Learning and Innovation.* Vol 2, Issue 2, pp 1-9.

[20] "Leadership by the New Generation." *MindTools.com.*

[21] "Leadership by the New Generation." *MindTools.com.*

[22] Denning, Steve. "The Key Missing Ingredient In Leadership Today." *www.Forbes.com.* 27 July 2012.

[23] Green, Holly. "Leadership: Then and Now." *www.Forbes.com.* 30 Aug 2011.

[23] Green, Holly. "Leadership: Then and Now." *www.Forbes.com.* 30 Aug 2011.

[24] "Lead Change Effectively." *DaleCarnegie.com.* 2014.

[25] Cole, Neil. "Old v. New Leadership: A Study in Contrasts." *CMAResources.Org.* 16 Nov 2012.

[26] Remarks by U.S. Permanent Representative to the United Nations, Ambassador Samantha Power, at the United Nations Association of the USA 2013 Global Leadership Awards, November 6, 2013.

[27] Hurd, Mark V. "Five Leadership Qualities Great Executives Must Have." *www.linkedin.com.*

[28] Green, Holly. "Leadership: Then and Now." *www.Forbes.com.* 30 Aug 2011.

[29] Pontrefact, Dan. *Flat Army: Creating a Connected and Engaged Organization.* Wiley: New York, March 2013.

[30] McKinney, Michael. "Leading Views: Pervasive Learning." *www.leadershipnow.com/leadingblog.* 15 Jan 2014.

[31] Ash, Katie. "Building a District Culture to Foster Innovation." *Education Week Magazine.* 2 Oct 2013.

[32] "The Evolution of Leadership." *MindResources Institute of Learning and Innovation.* Vol 2, Issue 2, pp 1-9.

³³ Crabtree, Steve. "Worldwide, 13% of Employees Are Engaged at Work." *Gallup Worldwide.* 8 Oct 2013.

³⁴ Crabtree, Steve. "Worldwide, 13% of Employees Are Engaged at Work." *Gallup Worldwide.* 8 Oct 2013.

³⁵ Economy, Peter. "7 Ways to Lead With Your Heart." *www.inc.com.* 14 Feb 2014.

³⁶ *Ibid.*

³⁷ Source: Gallup, n.d.

³⁸ Cataldo, Pat. "Focusing on Employee Engagement: How to Measure It *and* Improve It." *UNC Keenan-Flagler Business School.* Executive Development 2011.

³⁹ Sutton, Robert and Rao, Hayagreeva. "How do You Scale Excellence?" *www.gsb.stanford.edu/news.* 7 Jan 2014.

⁴⁰ Robison, Jennifer and Crabtree, Steve. "Engaged Workplaces are Engines of Job Creation." *Gallup Business Journal.* 8 Oct 2013.

⁴¹ Robison, Jennifer and Crabtree, Steve. "Engaged Workplaces are Engines of Job Creation." *Gallup Business Journal.* 8 Oct 2013.

⁴² Johnson, Patti. *"10 Trends Change Leaders Can't Ignore in 2014"* from *Make Waves: Be the One to Start Change at Work and in Life.* Boston: Bibliomotion Inc., 2014.

⁴³ "The Evolution of Leadership." *MindResources Institute of Learning and Innovation.* Vol 2, Issue 2, pp 1-9.

⁴⁴ Green, Holly. Leadership: Then and Now." *www.Forbes.com.* 30 Aug 2011.

⁴⁵ Ash, Katie. "Building a District Culture to Foster Innovation." *Education Week Magazine.* 2 Oct 2013.

⁴⁶ AchieveGlobal with Craig Perrin, Sharon Daniels et al. *Developing the 21ˢᵗ Century Leader.* Tampa, Florida: AchieveGlobal World Headquarters, 2010.

⁴⁷ Visconti, Luke. "Ask the White Guy: Why White Men Must Attend Diversity Training." www.diversityinc.com.

⁴⁸ Bush, Vanessa K., "The Cultural Connection." http://diversitywoman.com. 23 January 2011.

⁴⁹ Johnson, Patti. *"10 Trends Change Leaders Can't Ignore in 2014"* from *Make Waves: Be the One to Start Change at Work and in Life.* Boston: Bibliomotion Inc., 2014.

[50] Sutton, Robert and Rao, Hayagreeva. "How do You Scale Excellence?" *www.gsb.stanford.edu/news.* 7 Jan 2014.

[51] "The Insider: Susan Taylor Batten." *www.BlacksGiveBack.com.* 13 Feb 2013.

[52] Dunn, Andy and Ekiel, Erika Brown. "Passion is a Prerequisite." 11 Dec 2013. *www.gsb.stanford.edu/news.*

[53] "Building Better Business Relationships." *www.businessblogshub.com.* 6 Dec 2013.

[54] Benderev, Chris. "When Power Goes To Your Head, It May Shut Out Your Heart." NPR. 10 Aug 2013.

[55] Economy, Peter. "7 Ways to Lead With Your Heart." *www.inc.com.* 14 Feb 2014.

[56] "Can you Turn Someone On Your Team Into a Good Leader?" *www.businessblogshub.com.* 1 Oct 2013.

[57] Foer, Jonathan Safran. "How Not to Be Alone." *The New York Times,* Sunday Opinion. 8 June 2013.

[58] Richtel, Matt. "Attached to Technology and Paying the Price." *The New York Times.* 6 June 2010.

[59] Carr, Nicholas. *The Shallows.* New York: W.W. Norton and Co, 2010.

[60] Carr, Nicholas. *The Shallows.* New York: W.W. Norton and Co, 2010.

[61] Martinuzzi, Bruna. *The Leader as a Mensch: Become the Kind of Person Others Want to Follow.* Silicon Valley: Six Seconds Emotional Intelligence Press, 2009.

[62] "Building Better Business Relationships." *www.businessblogshub.com.* 6 Dec 2013.

[63] Economy, Peter. "7 Ways to Lead With Your Heart." *www.inc.com.* 14 Feb 2014.

[64] MacDonald, Matthew. "Leadership–Influencing Through Relationship." *BusinessBlogsHub.com.* May 2011.

[65] Hurd, Mark V. "Five Leadership Qualities Great Executives Must Have." 9 Dec 2013. *www.linkedin.com/post.*

[66] "Building Better Business Relationships." *www.businessblogshub.com.* 6 Dec 2013.

[67] Greer, Lindred. "Business Leaders Ignore Power Struggles at Their Organization's Risk." *www.gsb.stanford.edu.* 16 Jan 2014.

68 "Leadership by the New Generation: Bridging the Age Gap."
*www.mindtools.com.* MindTools.com. (Year). Article/Resource Title.
[Online]. Available from: http://www.mindtools.com/full-URL. [Accessed: Date].

69 Bowkett, Paul. "Customer Relationship Management: Five Tips for Building Stronger Customer Relationships."

70 Bowkett, Paul. "Customer Relationship Management: Five Tips for Building Stronger Customer Relationships."

71 Clark, Dorie. "How to Reinvent Yourself After 50." *HarvardBusinessReviewNetwork.* 13 Dec 2013.

72 Kwoh, Leslie and Korn, Lisa. "140 Characters of Risk: Some CEOs Fear Twitter." *The Wall Street Journal.* 26 Sept 2012.

73 "2013 CEO.Com Social CEO Report." *www.ceo.com.*

74 Kwoh, Leslie and Korn, Lisa. "140 Characters of Risk: Some CEOs Fear Twitter." *The Wall Street Journal.* 26 Sept 2012.

75 Frederickson, Lee, PhD. "The Bottom-Line Benefits of Blogging." *www.LeadershipCloseUp.com.* 3 April 2013.

76 Demartini, John. "On Inspired Leaders." *Business Brief Magazine/* bbrief.co.za.

77 Sutton, Robert and Rao, Hayagreeva. "How do You Scale Excellence." *www.gsb.stanford.edu/news.* 7 Jan 2014.

78 Stephenson, Carol, O.C. "How Leadership Has Changed." *Ivey Business Journal/From The Dean.* July-August 2011

79 Stephenson, Carol, O.C. "How Leadership Has Changed." *Ivey Business Journal/From The Dean.* July-August 2011

80 Tredgold, Gordon. "10 Things You Can Do to Improve Your Leadership Today." *www.leadership-principles.com.* 13 Feb 2014.

81 "Leadership by the New Generation: Bridging the Age Gap." *www.mindtools.com.* MindTools.com. (Year). Article/Resource Title.
[Online]. Available from: http://www.mindtools.com/full-URL. [Accessed: Date].

82 McDonald, Tim. "What a Homeless Man Taught Me About Leadership." *The Huffington Post.* 14 Feb 2014.

83 Alessandra, Tony and O'Connor, Michael. "The Platinum Rule: Discover the Four Basic Business Personalities and How They Can Lead You to Success." New York: Warner Business Books, 1998.

84 Alessadria, Tony. "The Platinum Rule."
*www.platinumrule.com/aboutpr.asp*

85 Alessadria, Tony. "The Platinum Rule."
*www.platinumrule.com/aboutpr.asp*

86 List Source: "Inside Amazon's Idea Machine." *Forbes.* 23 April 2012.

87 Spence, Rick. "Why Do We Need Leaders?" *www.profitguide.com.*
22 Aug 2011.

88 "The Evolution of Leadership." *MindResources Institute of Learning
and Innovation.* Vol 2, Issue 2, pp 1-9.

89 Callahan, Clinton. "Becoming a Leader to Change the World for the
Better." *www.radicalhonesty.com.* 26 Nov 2013.

90 Zmorenski, Debbie. "Why Leaders Must Have Vision."
*www.reliableplant.com.* 29 Jan 2009.

91 Zmorenski, Debbie. "Why Leaders Must Have Vision."
*www.reliableplant.com.* 29 Jan 2009.

92 Economy, Peter. "7 Ways to Lead With Your Heart." *www.inc.com.*
14 Feb 2014.

93 MacDonald, Matthew. "Leadership–Influencing Through
Relationships." *www.businessblogshub.com.* 6 May 2011.

94 Demartini, John. "On Inspired Leaders." *Business Brief Magazine/*
bbrief.co.za.

95 Economy, Peter. "7 Ways to Lead With Your Heart." *www.inc.com.*
14 Feb 2014.

96 Maslow, A.H. "A Theory of Human Motivation." *Psychological
Review,* 1943. *50*(4), 370-96.

97 Maslow, A. *Motivation and Personality.* New York: Harper, 1954. 91.

98 Maslow, A. *Motivation and Personality.* New York: Harper, 1954. 91.

99 Haudan, Jim. "Employee Engagement: Being Part of Something
Bigger than Yourself." *www.watercoolernewslettercom.* March/April 2014.

100 Sinek, Simon. *Start With Why: How Great Leaders Inspire Everyone
to Take Action.* New York: Penguin Group, 2009.

101 Zinsmeister, Sean. "Global Business Leadership."
*www.businessblogshub.com.* 15 Feb 2011.

102 Zinsmeister, Sean. "Global Business Leadership."
*www.businessblogshub.com.* 15 Feb 2011.

[103] Denning, Steve. "The Key Missing Ingredient In Leadership Today." *www.Forbes.com.* 27 July 2012.

[104] Haudan, Jim. "Employee Engagement: Being Part of Something Bigger than Yourself." *www.watercoolernewslettercom.* March/April 2014.

[105] Demartini, John. "On Inspired Leaders." *Business Brief Magazine/* bbrief.co.za.

[106] Tredgold, Gordon. "10 Things You Can Do to Improve Your Leadership Today." *www.leadership-principles.com.* 13 Feb 2014.

[107] Hurd, Mark V. "Five Leadership Qualities Great Executives Must Have." *www.linkedin.com/post.* 9 Dec 2013.

[108] Greenberg, Melanie. "Six Qualities Leaders Need to be Successful." *Psychology Today.* April 2012.

[109] Gallo, Carmine. "Seven Ways to Inspire Employees to Love Their Job." *Forbes.com.* 21 June 2013.

[110] Gallo, Carmine. "Seven Ways to Inspire Employees to Love Their Job." *Forbes.com.* 21 June 2013.

[111] Andersen, Erika. *Leading so People Will Follow.* New York: Wiley/Jossey-Bass, 2012.

[112] Andersen, Erika. "Passionate Leaders Aren't Loud—They're Deep." *www.forbes.com.* 11 June 2012.

[113] Stein, Joel. "Boringness: The Secret to Great Leadership." *Harvard Business Review Blog.* 18 May 2012.

[114] Stephenson, Carol, O.C. "How Leadership Has Changed." *Ivey Business Journal/From The Dean.* July-August 2011.

[115] Zmorenski, Debbie. "Why Leaders Must Have Vision." *www.reliableplant.com.* 29 Jan 2009.

[116] MacDonald, Matthew. "Leadership–Influencing Through Relationship." *BusinessBlogsHub.com.* May 2011.

[117] Tredgold, Gordon. *Leadership: It's a Marathon, Not a Sprint.* St. Albans, Hertsfordshire: Panoma Press, Nov 2013.

[118] Callahan, Clinton. "Becoming a Leader to Change the World for the Better." *www.radicalhonesty.com.* 26 Nov 2013.

[119] *ReliablePlant.com.*

[120] Zmorenski, Debbie. "Why Leaders Must Have Vision." *www.reliableplant.com.* 29 Jan 2009.

[121] "Can you Turn Someone On Your Team Into a Good Leader?" *www.businessblogshub.com.* 1 Oct 2013.

[122] Denning, Steve. "The Key Missing Ingredient In Leadership Today." *www.Forbes.com.* 27 July 2012.

[123] MacDonald, Matthew. "Leadership–Influencing Through Relationship." *BusinessBlogsHub.com.* May 2011.

[124] DiMattia, Ernie. "Leadership vs. Management." *Library Journal.* 11 March 2013.

[125] Sutton, Robert and Rao, Hayagreeva. "How do You Scale Excellence?" *www.gsb.stanford.edu/news.* 7 Jan 2014.

[126] Hurd, Mark V. "Five Leadership Qualities Great Executives Must Have." *www.linkedin.com/post.* 9 Dec 2013.

[127] Hurd, Mark V. "Five Leadership Qualities Great Executives Must Have." *www.linkedin.com/post.* 9 Dec 2013.

[128] "Can One Person Make a Difference?" *www.businessblogshub.com.* February 2014.

[129] Sutton, Robert and Rao, Hayagreeva. "How do You Scale Excellence?" *www.gsb.stanford.edu/news.* 7 Jan 2014.

[130] Greer, Lindred. "Business Leaders Ignore Power Struggles at Their Organization's Risk." *Stanford GSB Review.* 16 Jan 2014.

[131] Tredgold, Gordon. "10 Things You Can Do to Improve Your Leadership Today." *www.leadership-principles.com.* 13 Feb 2014.

[132] Johnson, Patti. *"10 Trends Change Leaders Can't Ignore in 2014"* from *Make Waves: Be the One to Start Change at Work and in Life.* Boston: Bibliomotion Inc., 2014.

[133] Greathouse, John. "23 Leadership Tips from Oprah Winfrey." *Forbes Magazine.* 27 Sept 2012.

[134] Nesheim, John L. *The Power of Unfair Advantage.* New York: Free Press, 2005.

[135] Nesheim, John L. *The Power of Unfair Advantage.* New York: Free Press, 2005.

[136] Barr, Corbett. "The Ultimate Guide to Finding your Unique Selling position. *http://fizzle.co/sparkline/unique-selling-proposition.* 2014.

[137] Flynn, Pat. "Are You Taking Advantage of Your Unfair Advantage?" *www.smartpassiveincome.com.* 16 April 2013.

[138] Johnson, Patti. *Make Waves: Be the One to Start Change at Work and in Life.* Boston: Bibliomotion Inc., 2014.

[139] Dunn, Andy and Ekiel, Erika Brown. "Passion is a Prerequisite." 11 Dec 2013. *www.gsb.stanford.edu/news.*

[140] CBS News. "Facebook: One Social Graph to Rule Them All?" 21 April 2010. *www.cbsnews.com.*

[141] Dickinson, Boonsri. "So What the Heck is the 'Social Graph' Facebook Keeps Talking About?" *BusinessInsider.com.* 2 Mar 2012.

[142] Griggs, Brandon. "Biz Stone: Humans can Outsmart the Internet." *Cnn.com.* 12 March 2014.

[143] Segall, Laurie. "Twitter co-founder Biz Stone launches New App." *www.money.cnn.com.* 7 Jan 2014.

[144] Heilpern, John. "Out to Lunch with Biz Stone." *Vanity Fair.* April 2014.

[145] Griggs, Brandon. "Biz Stone: Humans can Outsmart the Internet." *Cnn.com.* 12 March 2014.

[146] Mendoza, Dorinne. "Biz Stone: What Jelly Can Do For You." *www.CNN.com/tech.i* 8 Jan 2014.

[147] Johnson, Patti. *"10 Trends Change Leaders Can't Ignore in 2014"* from *Make Waves: Be the One to Start Change at Work and in Life.* Boston: Bibliomotion Inc., 2014.

[148] Johnson, Patti. *"10 Trends Change Leaders Can't Ignore in 2014"* from *Make Waves: Be the One to Start Change at Work and in Life.* Boston: Bibliomotion Inc., 2014.

[149] http://talent.linkedin.com/blog/index.php/2014/02/mobile-recruiting-statistics-infographic

[150] Ignatova, Maria. *Mobile Recruiting Playbook.* LinkedIn Talent Solutions. 5 February 2014.

[151] Cohen, Jason. "Real Unfair Advantages." *www.blog.asmartbear.com.* 19 July 2010.

[152] Stone, Biz. *Things a Little Bird told Me.* New York: Grand Central Publishing, 2014.

[153] MacDonald, Matthew. "Leadership–Influencing Through Relationship." *BusinessBlogsHub.com.* May 2011.

[154] Hurd, Mark V. "Five Leadership Qualities Great Executives Must Have." *www.linkedin.com.* 9 Dec 2013.

[155] Hurd, Mark V. "Five Leadership Qualities Great Executives Must Have." *www.linkedin.com.* 9 Dec 2013.

[156] Hurd, Mark V. "Five Leadership Qualities Great Executives Must Have." *www.linkedin.com.* 9 Dec 2013.

[157] Johnson, Patti. *"10 Trends Change Leaders Can't Ignore in 2014"* from *Make Waves: Be the One to Start Change at Work and in Life.* Boston: Bibliomotion Inc., 2014.

[158] Dunn, Andy and Ekiel, Erika Brown. "Passion is a Prerequisite." 11 Dec 2013. *www.gsb.stanford.edu/news.*

[159] Stephenson, Carol, O.C. "How Leadership Has Changed." *Ivey Business Journal/From The Dean.* July-August 2011.

[160] Stephenson, Carol, O.C. "How Leadership Has Changed." *Ivey Business Journal/From The Dean.* July-August 2011.

[161] "Lead Change Effectively." *DaleCarnegie.com.* 2014.

[162] Stone, Biz. *Things a Little Bird told Me.* New York: Grand Central Publishing, 2014.

[163] Stephenson, Carol, O.C. "How Leadership Has Changed." *Ivey Business Journal/From The Dean.* July-August 2011.

[164] McKinney, Michael. "How do Leaders Gain Deep Insights?" *www.leadershipnow.com.* 3 Jan 2014.

[165] Stephenson, Carol, O.C. "How Leadership Has Changed." *Ivey Business Journal/From The Dean.* July-August 2011.

[166] Sutton, Robert and Rao, Hayagreeva. "How do You Scale Excellence?" *www.gsb.stanford.edu/news.* 7 Jan 2014.

[167] Greer, Lindred. "Business Leaders Ignore Power Struggles at Their Organization's Risk." *Stanford GSB Review.* 16 Jan 2014.

[168] Tredgold, Gordon. "10 Things You Can Do to Improve Your Leadership Today." *www.leadership-principles.com.* 13 Feb 2014.

[169] Riggio, Ronald, PhD. "Top 6 Reasons Why People Hate Their Bosses. *Psychology Today.* 19 February 2013.

[170] Kerpen, Dave. *Likeable Leadership.* New York: Likeable Publishing, October 2013.

[171] Kerpin, Carrie. "Professional Women and Likeability: Does it Matter?" *www.forbes.com.* 1 July 2013.

[172] Clark, Dorie. "How to Become a More Likeable Leader." *www.forbes.com.* 25 Nov 2013.

[173] Tankersley, Jim. "What Drives Mary Barra." *Stanford Alumni Magazines.* Sept-Oct 2011.

[174] Engelmeier, Shirley. "Did Mary Barra's Inclusive Leadership Style Propel Her to The Top?" *Industry Week.* 22 Jan 2014.

[175] Coleman, John. "Leadership is Not a Solitary Task." *Harvard Business Review.* 5 Feb 2014.

◆ ◆ ◆ ◆ ◆ ◆

www.ingramcontent.com/pod-product-compliance
Lightning Source LLC
Chambersburg PA
CBHW071227210326
41597CB00016B/1978